《中国节庆文化》丛书
编委会名单

顾　问
　　史蒂文·施迈德　　冯骥才　　周明甫
　　黄忠彩　　武翠英　　王国泰

主　编
　　李　松

副主编
　　张　刚　　彭新良

编　委（按姓氏笔画排列）
　　王学文　　田　阡　　邢　莉　　齐勇锋
　　李　旭　　李　松　　杨正文　　杨海周
　　张　刚　　张　勃　　张　跃　　张　暖
　　金　蕾　　赵学玉　　萧　放　　彭新良

List of Members of Editorial Board
of *Chinese Festival Culture Series*

中国节庆文化丛书

Chinese Festival Culture Series

The Festival of
February the Second

主　编　李　松

副主编　张　刚　彭新良

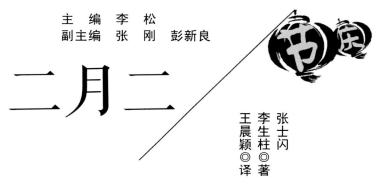

二月二

王晨颖◎译　李生柱◎著　张士闪

全 国 百 佳 图 书 出 版 单 位

ARTTIME　时代出版传媒股份有限公司

安 徽 人 民 出 版 社

图书在版编目(CIP)数据

二月二:汉英对照/张士闪,李生柱著;王晨颖译.—合肥:安徽人民出版社,2014.1
(中国节庆文化丛书/李松,张刚,彭新良主编)

ISBN 978-7-212-07070-0

Ⅰ.①二… Ⅱ.①张… ②李… ③王… Ⅲ.①节日—风俗习惯—中国—汉、英 Ⅳ.①K892.1

中国版本图书馆 CIP 数据核字(2013)第 315280 号

Zhongguo Jieqing Wenhua Congshu   Eryueer

中国节庆文化丛书　**二月二**

李　松　**主编**　张　刚　彭新良　**副主编**

张士闪　李生柱　**著**　王晨颖　**译**

出　版　人:朱寒冬　　　　　　　　　图书策划:胡正义　丁怀超　李　旭
责任编辑:朱　虹　李　莉　　　　　　装帧设计:宋文岚

出版发行:时代出版传媒股份有限公司 http://www.press-mart.com
　　　　　安徽人民出版社 http://www.ahpeople.com
　　　　　合肥市政务文化新区翡翠路 1118 号出版传媒广场八楼
　　　　　邮编:230071
　　　　　营销部电话:0551-63533258　0551-63533292(传真)
制　　　版:合肥市中旭制版有限责任公司
印　　　制:安徽新华印刷股份有限公司

开本:710×1010　1/16　　　印张:12.5　　　字数:220 千
版次:2014 年 3 月第 1 版　　2016 年 7 月第 4 次印刷

标准书号:ISBN 978-7-212-07070-0　　定价:24.00 元

Our Common Days

(Preface)

The most important day for a person in a year is his or her birthday, and the most important days for all of us are the festivals. We can say that the festivals are our common days.

Festivals are commemorating days with various meanings. There are national, ethnic and religious festivals, such as the National Day and Christmas Day, and some festivals for certain groups, such as the Women's Day, the Children's Day, the Mothers' Day and the Labor Day. There are some other festivals closely related to our lives. These festivals have long histories and different customs that have been passed on from one generation to another. There are also different traditional festivals. China is a country full of 56 ethnic groups, and all of the ethnic groups are collectively called the Chinese Nation. Some traditional festivals are common to all people of the Chinese Nation, and some others are unique to certain ethnic groups. For example, the Spring Festival, the Mid-Autumn Day, the Lantern Festival, the Dragon Boat Festival, the Tomb-Sweeping Day and the Double-Ninth Day are common festivals to all of the Chinese people. On the other hand, the New Year of the Qiang Ethnic (a World Cultural Heritage), for example, is a unique

我们共同的日子

（代序）

个人一年一度最重要的日子是生日，大家一年一度最重要的日子是节日。节日是大家共同的日子。

节日是一种纪念日，内涵多种多样。有民族的、国家的、宗教的，比如国庆节、圣诞节等。有某一类人的，如妇女、儿童、劳动者的，这便是妇女节、儿童节、劳动节等。也有与人们的生活生产密切相关的，这类节日历史悠久，很早就形成了一整套人们约定俗成、代代相传的节日习俗，这是一种传统的节日。传统节日也多种多样。中国是个多民族国家，有五十六个民族，统称中华民族。传统节日有全民族共有的，也有某个民族特有的。比如春节、中秋节、元宵节、端午节、清明节、重阳节等，就为中华民族所共用和共享；世界文化遗产羌年就为羌族独有和独享。各民族这样的节日很多。

传统节日是在漫长的农耕时代形成的。农耕时代生产与生活、人与自然的关系十分密切。人们或为了感恩于大自然的恩赐，或为了庆祝辛苦劳作换来的收获，或为了激发生命的活力，或为了加强人际的亲情，经过长期相互认同，最终约定俗成，渐渐把一年中某一天确定为节日，并创造了十分完整又严格的节俗，如仪式、庆典、规制、禁忌，乃至特定的游艺、装饰与食品，来把节日这天演化成一个独具内涵和迷人的日子。更重要的是，人们在每一个传统的节日里，还把共同的生活理想、人间愿望与审美追求融入节日的内涵与种种仪式中。因此，它是中华民族世间理想与生活愿望极致的表现。可以说，我们的传统——精神文化传统，往往就是依靠这代代相传的一年一度的节日继承下来的。

festival to the Qiang Ethnic Group, and there are many festivals celebrated only by minorities in China.

The traditional festivals are formed throughout the long agrarian age, during which the relationships between life and production and between the people and the nature were very close. To express the gratitude to the nature for its gifts, or celebrate the harvests from hard works, or stimulate the vitality of life, or strengthen the relationships among people, people would determine one day in a year as a festival with complete and strict customs, such as ceremonies, rules and taboos, special activities, decorations and foods to make the festival a day with unique meanings and charms. More importantly, people would integrate their good wishes into the meanings and ceremonies of the festivals. Therefore, the festivals could represent the ideals and wishes of the people in the best way. It is safe to say that our traditions, more specifically, our spiritual and cultural traditions, are inherited through the festivals year by year.

However, since the 20th century, with the transition from the agricultural civilization to the industrial civilization, the cultural traditions formed during the agrarian age have begun to collapse. Especially in China, during the process of opening up in the past 100 years, the festival culture, especially the festival culture in cities, has been impacted by the modern civilization and foreign cultures. At present, the Chinese people have felt that the traditional festivals are leaving away day by day so that some worries are produced about this. With the diminishing of the traditional festivals, the traditional spirits carried by them will also disappear. However, we are not just watching them disappearing, but actively dealing with them, which could fully represent the self-consciousness of the Chinese people in terms of culture.

In those ten years, with the fully launching of the folk culture heritage rescue program of China, and the promotion of the application for national non-material cultural heritage list, more attention has been paid to the traditional festivals, some of which have been added to the central cultural heritage list. After that, in 2006, China has determined that the second Saturday of June of each year shall be the Cultural Heritage Day, and in 2007, the State Council added three important festivals, namely the Tomb-sweeping Day, the Dragon Boat Festival and the Mid-Autumn Day, as the legal holidays. These decisions have showed that our government

然而，自从二十世纪整个人类进入了由农耕文明向工业文明的过渡，农耕时代形成的文化传统开始瓦解。尤其是中国，在近百年由封闭走向开放的过程中，节日文化——特别是城市的节日文化受到现代文明与外来文化的冲击。当下人们已经鲜明地感受到传统节日渐行渐远，并为此产生忧虑。传统节日的淡化必然使其中蕴含的传统精神随之涣散。然而，人们并没有坐等传统的消失，主动和积极地与之应对。这充分显示了当代中国人在文化上的自觉。

近十年，随着中国民间文化遗产抢救工程的全面展开，国家非物质文化遗产名录申报工作的有力推动，传统节日受到关注，一些重要的传统节日列入了国家文化遗产名录。继而，2006年国家将每年六月的第二个周六确定为"文化遗产日"；2007年国务院决定将三个中华民族的重要节日——清明节、端午节和中秋节列为法定放假日。这一重大决定，表现了国家对公众的传统文化生活及其传承的重视与尊重，同时也是保护节日文化遗产十分必要的措施。

节日不放假必然直接消解了节日文化，放假则是恢复节日传统的首要条件。但放假不等于远去的节日立即就会回到身边。节日与假日的不同是因为节日有特定的文化内容与文化形式。那么，重温与恢复已经变得陌生的传统节日习俗则是必不可少的了。

千百年来，我们的祖先从生活的愿望出发，为每一个节日都创造出许许多多美丽又动人的习俗。这种愿望是理想主义的，所以节日习俗是理想的；愿望是情感化的，所以节日习俗也是情感化的；愿望是美好的，所以节日习俗是美的。人们用合家团聚的年夜饭迎接新年；把天上的明月化为手中甜甜的月饼，来象征人间的团圆；在严寒刚刚消退、万物复苏的早春，赶到野外去打扫墓地，告慰亡灵，

emphasizes and respects the traditional cultural activities and their heritages. Meanwhile, these are important measures to protect festival cultural heritages.

Festivals without holidays will directly harm the festival culture. Holiday is the most important condition for the recovery of a festival, but holiday does not mean that the festival will come back immediately. Festivals are different from holidays because festivals have unique cultural contents and forms. Therefore, it will be necessary to review and recover the customs of the traditional festivals that have become strange to us.

For thousands of years, our ancestors created beautiful and moving customs for each festival based on their best wishes. The customs are ideal, since the wishes are ideal. The customs are emotional, since the wishes are emotional. The customs are beautiful, since the wishes are beautiful. We have the family reunion dinner to receive a new year. We make moon cakes according to the shape of the moon in the mid-autumn to symbolize the reunion of our family. We visit the tombs of our ancestors in the early spring and go outing to beautiful and green hills to express our grief. These beautiful festival customs have offered us great comfort and peace for generations.

To ethnic minorities, their unique festivals are of more importance, since these festivals bear their common memories and represent their spirits, characters and identities.

Who ever can say that the traditional customs are out of date? If we have forgotten these customs, we should review them. The review is not imitating the customs of our ancients, but experiencing the spirits and emotions of the traditions with our heart.

During the course of history, customs are changing, but the essence of the national tradition will not change. The tradition is to constantly pursue a better life, to be thankful to the nature and to express our best wishes for family reunion and the peace of the world.

This is the theme of our festivals, and the reason and purpose of this series of books.

The planning and compiling of the series is unique. All of the festivals are held once a year. Since China is a traditional agricultural society,

表达心中的缅怀，同时戴花插柳，踏青春游，亲切地拥抱大地山川……这些诗意化的节日习俗，使我们一代代人的心灵获得了美好的安慰与宁静。

对于少数民族来说，他们特有的节日的意义则更加重要。节日还是他们民族集体记忆的载体、共同精神的依托、个性的表现、民族身份之所在。

谁说传统的习俗过时了？如果我们淡忘了这些习俗，就一定要去重温一下传统。重温不是表象地模仿古人的形式，而是用心去体验传统中的精神与情感。

在历史的进程中，习俗是在不断变化的，但民族传统的精神本质不应变。这传统就是对美好生活不懈的追求，对大自然的感恩与敬畏，对家庭团圆与世间和谐永恒的企望。

这便是我们节日的主题，也是这套节庆丛书编写的根由与目的。

这套书的筹划独具匠心。所有节日都是一年一次。由于我国为传统农耕社会，所以生活与生产同步，节日与大自然的节气密切相关。本丛书以一年的春、夏、秋、冬四个时间板块，将纷繁的传统节日清晰有序地排列开来，又总揽成书，既包括全民族共有的节日盛典，也把少数民族重要的节日遗产纳入其中，以周详的文献和生动的传说，将每个节日的源起、流布与习俗，亦图亦文、有滋有味地娓娓道来。一节一册，单用方便，放在一起则是中华民族传统节日的一部全书，既有知识性、资料性、工具性，又有阅读性和趣味性。这样一套丛书不仅是对我国传统节日的一次总结，也是对传统节日文化富于创意的弘扬。

　　我读了书稿，心生欣喜，因序之。

冯骥才

2013.12.25

the life is synchronized with production, and the festivals are closely relevant to the climates. In this series, all of the traditional festivals in China will be introduced in the order of the four seasons, covering the common festivals as well as important ethnic festivals that have been listed as cultural heritages. All of the festivals are described in detail with texts and images to introduce their origins, customs and distribution. Each book of the series is used to introduce one festival so that it is convenient to read individually and it may be regarded as a complete encyclopedia if connected with each other. Therefore, it is not only intellectual, informative and instrumental, but also readable and interesting. The series could be used as a tool book or read for leisure. It is not only the summary of the traditional festivals of our country, but an innovative promotion of our traditional festival culture.

I felt very delighted after reading the manuscript, so I wrote this preface.

Feng Jicai

December 25th, 2013

目　录 / Contents

Foreword

The Festival of February 2nd arrives when the joyous mood of Chinese New Year still lingers on. It falls on the second day of the second lunar month. During the time of Waking of Insects, when the earth begins to breathe, and all living creatures wake up from hibernation. It is believed that dragons are the head of all insects, bringing clouds to the sky and rains to the earth. On February 2nd, when dragons raise their heads, spring is back to earth with more rains, and farmers begin to pray for a good harvest year. The day is celebrated as a festival for dragons, such is the reason why it is also called "Day of the God in the East ", "Day of the Spring Dragon" and "Day of Dragon Head".

A number of celebration activities on February 2nd are related to dragons. As a totem of Chinese people, dragons are worshipped in China throughout all ages till this day. The image of dragon varies for different people some are kind-hearted, some naughty, some lazy and some extremely ferocious. During the February 2nd Festival, the dragon in

前　言

过年的喜庆还余味缭绕，二月二佳节又如期而至。二月二因节期在农历二月初二而得名。此时，正值惊蛰前后，地气通透，万物复苏，经过漫长冬眠的动物日渐活跃。民间认为，龙是百虫之首，龙王能行云布雨，"二月二，龙抬头"象征着春回大地，雨水增多，农家生活燃起了希望。这就是为什么二月二是龙的节日，称为"青龙节""春龙节""龙头节"等节日的原因。

二月二的许多节俗活动，的确都与龙有关。龙是中华民族的图腾，其影响古往今来，贯穿大江南北。然而，在民众心目中，并非千龙一面，有的龙善良，有的龙调皮，有的龙懒惰，还有的龙极为凶恶。在二月二节日期间，人们对这主管雨水之神，或者崇拜有加，以香烛供品进行祭祀，或者设下种种禁忌，避免惹其不高兴。而对于那些懒龙、恶龙就不客气了，会想出各种法儿刺激它，如敲击梁头（敲龙头）、吃炒豆（崩龙眼）、吃面（吃龙须）、吃饺子（吃龙耳）、吃面饼（扯龙鳞）等，促其兴云布雨，令风调雨顺、五谷丰登，千万不能耽误职司。民间流传着这样一首儿歌："二月二，龙抬头；大仓满，小仓流。"诸多敬畏龙王的节俗，并非是逢旱逢涝之时的功利性举动，而是对抽象之龙的体贴、呵护或调侃、戏耍，寄托着人们祈龙赐福、保佑风调雨顺、五谷丰登的强烈愿望。

传统农业的命脉在于雨水，更在于土地，于是祭祀土地的仪式也被安排在二月二这天。在我国很多地方，二月二节日期间都时兴种种土地崇拜的仪

charge of rain and water is worshipped with joss sticks, incenses and candles as tributes, or carefully guarded in case it is offended. For those lazy and evil ones, people would irritate and tame them, by hitting attic beam (homophonic phrase as hitting dragons' heads in Chinese), eating stir-fried green beans (as they look like dragons' eyes), noodles (dragons' beards), dumplings (dragons' ears) and pancakes (dragons' skin), so that they will bring a favorable weather for harvest in the future, instead of neglecting their duties. A folk song goes as the following: On February 2nd when dragons raise their heads, barns are full with grains and mouths are fed. All these customs and activities in veneration of the dragon king are not considered as a pray for temporary protection against droughts and floods, but as people's deep concern and playful love for the abstract image of dragon, and their desire for the blessings that dragons bring a good harvest.

Water is the lifeblood for traditional agriculture, so is the soil. Therefore, the sacrifice ritual to the god of the earth is also arranged on February 2nd. Such a ritual is celebrated in many places of China to express people's gratitude and awe towards the great nature, as well as their expectations for a

harvest year. A series of rituals and activities, led by "Dragon head raising" and "earth worshipping", are carried out to celebrate the day of February 2nd, which reflects the agriculture experiences observed and collected by generations of farmers, and embodies their lively life expectations and ideals.

The Day of February 2nd roots from traditional agriculture civilization and marks the end of January and the beginning of a year's farming work. When the day of dragons raising their heads arrives, the whole Spring Festival Holiday comes to an end, people return to their daily farming and a busy season of spring ploughing begins.

February 2nd is a typical festival in spring. In the second month of the year, warm wind from southeast blows away the severe coldness, and nature wakes up from its winter dream. Trees and flowers unfold their buds, and insects are ready to come out. An inspiring warmth and vitality of spring take place of the chilling and awful winter as a response to people's life experience. At the end of the Spring Festival, people find it hard to say goodbye to all those leisure activities and happy reunions in the holiday time, and cherish their time spent in family trifles and with everything in their

式，表达感恩土地、敬畏大自然、期望农业丰收的情感。在二月二节俗中，以"龙抬头"和"祭土地神"为核心的一系列民俗仪式活动，既传达了民众长期观察的农业经验，又积淀着其活泼的生活期望与生命理想。

二月二既是在传统农业文明的土壤中孕育而生，也是一年一度的农事活动的启动标志，是"出正月"的象征。到了"龙抬头"之日，整个年节就算结束，人们要从过年期间香烟缭绕的氛围中重新回到农家日常生活的轨道，新一年的春耕大忙宣告开始。

二月二又是一个典型的春天节日。仲春二月，东南风徐徐吹来，带来阵阵暖流，严寒的威势逐渐减弱，自然万物开始复苏。树木花草抽发新芽，沉睡的百虫蠢蠢欲动，大自然以鼓舞人心的温暖和生机取代冬日的严寒和肃杀，这恰与民众的生命体验形成呼应。人们总是在年节快结束的时候，特别留恋这段将逝的休闲欢聚时光，并由此对家庭生活乃至家园中的一切充满感怀。二月二的一些特有节俗与此密切相关，如敲门梁、扫墙角、敲打屋梁、不动刀剪等。二月二节俗，意在提醒人们体察自然的萌动、敬畏自然、体贴生灵。

二月二是一个平等温馨的节日。曾几何时，二月二的城乡大街上处处洋溢着炒豆的馨香，再贫困的家户也能感染到这种节日的喜庆。一样的节期，大致一样的饮食，体现了一种众生平等的思想，是对平时社区生活中贫富、贵贱等差序格局的弥合。

在传统乡村社会中，二月二是欢快的。伴随着红红的炉火，滚烫的豆子在一口大铁锅里噼啪作响，馋嘴的孩子们在一旁转来转去，妇女们从容不迫地拉呱谈笑，回味刚刚过去的年节，交流新的一年的打算。这种邻里间亲热互助的温馨画面，会永久地烙印在童年的脑海里，至耄耋之年仍难忘怀。二月二还是一种亲情的体验与交流，这天出

house or garden. Some customs of February 2nd are especially related to such feelings, for example, knocking on the door beams, sweeping the corners of the house and non-touching knives or scissors. These customs all intend to remind people of their close relationship with nature, and of the respect and thoughtfulness they should hold for it.

February 2nd is a cozy and sweet holiday, when the delicious smell of frying beans drifts in all streets and lanes; even the most impoverished family is cheered up by the festival atmosphere. People poor or rich all share the same day of celebration and enjoy similar festival food, which represents a pursuit of human equality under a social hierarchy system of prejudice and oppression.

In traditional country life, February 2nd is a joyous day. Accompanied by the bright hearth fire, sizzling beans dance up and down in the cauldron, sweat walk back and forth and their mothers chatting about the passing holiday and their plans for the new year easily. A picture of friendly neighborhood stays in a child's memory for all his life, and will still be vivid when he reaches his seventies or eighties. February 2nd is also a day to rejuvenate family ties when married daughters come back to their parents, as an old saying goes, "girls are coming home on the second day of February, otherwise the parents are left heartbroken." Due to the custom of patrilocal residence, girls live with the family of her husband when she gets married; therefore, coming back to the parental home becomes a revisit to the life and people she was familiar with since her childhood and a spiritual return after years of being away from home. Only regular visits can fill up the gap of distance and bring the peace of mind back to life. The Day of February 2nd is not only about kinship tied by blood and marriage, but also about social relationship that needs regular refreshing. During the holiday season, neighbors send condiments and beans to each other as presents, thus a nice custom of "courtesy calls for reciprocity" is formed in this way, representing a harmonious neighborhood relationship of mutual help and benefit.

Following the spring Festival of New Year, the festival of February 2nd embodies people's collective wisdom and carries on their moral ideas, spiritual pursuits and value system. A rich variety of festival activities and customs implies the philosophy and awareness of life. By celebrating February 2nd, we are blessed with a more colorful life and a wiser mind.

嫁的闺女要回娘家，"二月二接宝贝，谁家不接掉眼泪"。在"从夫居"的社会模式中，回娘家是出嫁女子对娘家人思念的消解，是对原有生活空间和社会网络的重温，也是精神漂泊岁月中的翩然回归。唯其定期往来，遂对人生更觉一份踏实。当然，二月二不止协调基于血缘和姻缘而形成的亲属关系，还是对基于地缘而形成的社会关系的定期刷新。节日期间，邻里间要互相馈赠料豆等食品，并由此而形成了社区里礼尚往来的良好风俗，体现的是邻里之间互助互惠的和谐关系。

作为年的尾巴，二月二的设置积聚着民众的集体智慧，承载着他们千百年来形成的道德观念、精神需求、价值体系等，丰富的节俗中寓含着民众的生活逻辑和生命意识。过一回传统的二月二，我们的生活会更丰富，精神会更丰满。

第一章

从农事说源流

作为我国重要的传统节日之一，二月二历经千百年传承至今，曾有"龙抬头""青龙节""春龙节""龙头节""雨节""花朝节""开春节""震天节""中和节""土地公公日""伯公生日""填仓节""上工日"等别名。我国地域广袤，二月二在不同地域有着不同的节俗表现，至今在众多民族的日常生活中仍有着重要影响。

Chapter One

Agriculture: Origin of the Festival

As one of the essential traditional festivals in China, the Festival of February 2nd was celebrated thousands of years ago, as it is in the modern society. It has many names other than this one, such as "Dragon Head Raising Day", "Day of the God in the East", "Day of the Spring Dragon", "Day of Dragon Head", "Day of Rains", "Birthday of Flowers", "Day of Spring Beginning", "Sky Awakening Day", "Day of Balance","Birthday of Local God of Land", "Grain Barn Filling Day" and even "Working Day". China's massive land brings about the regional differences in celebrating the Day of February 2nd, which still influence the daily life of various peoples in many ways.

1

复合的二月二
A Melting-Pot of Festivals

Of all the traditional festivals, the Day of February 2nd is a late comer, as it is not until the Tang Dynasty (608—917) people begin to observe the day. But the origin of the Day can be traced back to the Day of Waking of Insects and Spring Earth Day in the Pre-Qin Period. The Day of February 2nd is just like a melting-pot that integrates a variety of festivals taking place in February, such as the Day of Waking of Insects, Spring Earth Day, Dragon Head Day, Day of Balance and the Birthday of Flowers. These festivals died out during the long stretch of history as their cultural elements and customs were assimilated, and finally, the Day of February 2nd is established.

1.The Day of Dragon Head Raising

Why do people name February 2nd as the Day of Dragon Head Raising? There are many legends

在中国传统节日的大家庭中，二月二是形成较晚的一个，学界一般认为其节期定型于唐朝。但二月二节日的雏形，可以追溯到先秦时期的惊蛰节、春社日等。其实，二月二是一个复合的节日，自古及今融汇了仲春二月的"惊蛰节""春社日""龙头节""中和节""花朝节"等。在历史长河的淘洗中，这些节日逐渐消退，最终都融合在二月二节日中。

一、龙抬头节

关于"二月二，龙抬头"的来历，民间有很多美丽的传说。有一则传说是这样讲述的：东海龙王有一个美貌如花的小女儿，生于二月初二日。有一天，小龙女悄悄溜出龙宫来到人间，正赶上人间大旱，庄稼焦黄，草木干枯。龙女见状，顿生怜悯之心。于是她从随身带的锦囊里取出一把红豆，向田地里一撒，天空中立刻浓云密布，电闪雷鸣，下起了大雨。雨后，方圆几百里的庄稼全都长得绿油油的。龙王得知此事后非常恼怒，认为龙女私自降雨，大逆不道，便将龙女逐出龙宫，永不相认。龙母非常思念她的小女儿，每到小龙女的生日二月初二这一天，她总要浮出水面，抬头眺望，痛哭一场。她的哭声变成了雷声，她的眼泪变成了大雨，春雷春雨给大地带来了生机，给农家带来了好年景的盼头。这便是"二月二，龙抬头"的来历。①

about it. One of them goes like this: the Dragon King of East Sea has a beautiful daughter, who was born on February 2nd. One day the young princess slipped out of the Dragon Palace and came to the mortal world, where people were suffering from a severe drought. The princess felt sad when she saw those withered crops and grasses scorched in the fields. She took out a handful of red beans from the kits she brought along with her, and scattered them into the fields. Suddenly, clouds began to gather in the sky. Lightening flashed and thunder rumbled, and there came the downpour of rain. When the rain finally stopped, the crops were all lightened up by a beautiful color of green. The Dragon King was outrageous when he learnt what his daughter had done in the mortal world. He believed that it is an offense against rules as the princess made the rain without his permission. As a result, the dragon princess was driven out of the palace as a punishment by her father. Her mother missed her so much that on her birthday, February 2nd, the queen came out of the water and raised her head to look up to the sky and cry her sorrows out. Her cry turned into the thunder and her tears the heavy rain, and thus the spring thunder and rain bringing life to earth and good hope of harvest for the famers. That's how the Day of Dragon Head Raising comes into being.①

①杨琳：《"二月二"风俗谈》，《寻根》2009年第1期。

①Yang Lin: *Customs on the Day of February 2nd*, *Root Exploration* 2009, issue 1.

2. The Day of the Waking of Insects

The Day of the Waking of Insects is one of the 24 solar terms. It falls on March 5th or 6th, when the sun reaches a celestial longitude of 345 degree. The day also reflects natural phonological phenomenon, which means that the thunders in spring wake up the insects from their hibernation.

On the Day of the Waking of Insects, when snakes, insects, rats and ants all wake up by the thunders and frequent the households for food, people would try to repel these unwanted visitors by all means. Sun Simiao, a well-known doctor in Tang Dynasty, emphasized in his *Phenology of Lunar Months* the custom of spreading ash "On the Waking of the Insects Day, households can get rid of insects and ants by spreading ash outside their doors."

二、惊蛰节

惊蛰是二十四节气之一，每年3月5日或6日，太阳到达黄经345度时为"惊蛰"。惊蛰是反映自然物候现象的一个节气，意为春雷始鸣，惊醒蛰伏于地下冬眠的昆虫。

惊蛰之时，冬眠中的蛇虫鼠蚁应春雷声而起，四处觅食，往往有害于人类，因此古时惊蛰当日，人们会想方设法予以驱赶。唐代孙思邈《千金月令》则格外强调惊蛰日的撒灰之俗："惊蛰日，取石灰糁门限外，可绝虫蚁。"惊蛰日撒灰驱虫的做法可说是二月二撒灰节俗的前身。显然，二月二与惊蛰节期相邻，当惊蛰融入了二月二，形形色色的驱虫方式自然就成为后世二月二节俗的核心内容之一了。

三、春社日

社日是中国古代仲春时节的重要节日，源于上古时期先民对土地的崇拜。"社"即"土"。《说文》曰："社，地主也。"社日就是祭祀土地神的日子。古时，祭祀社神一般是在春秋两季分别举行，有"春祈秋报"之说。汉代以前只有春社，没有秋社，而且春社祭祀没有固定日期，后来逐步确定立春后第五个戊日①为春社节，立秋后的第五个戊日为秋社节。

春社日是人们祭祀土谷神以祈求风调雨顺、人

---

①古人认为五行为水、火、木、金、土，与天干甲、乙、丙、丁、戊相对应，戊对应土，故社日以戊日为期。

This practice can be considered as the predecessor of the custom of spreading ash on the day of February 2nd. It is evident that when the Day of February 2nd assimilates customs of the Waking of the Insects Day, a variety of methods to expel insects become an essential part of the customs.

3.Spring Earth Day

Spring Earth Day is a major festival in the middle of spring in ancient China, which derives from our ancestors' worship of the earth. In *Origin of Chinese Characters*, "*She* is the god of the earth." Earth Day is the day to worship the God of Earth. In ancient times, the rituals of offering sacrifices to the God of Earth was often held in spring and autumn, which is often called "praying in spring and reporting in autumn". Before Han Dynasty, the worship ritual only took place in spring and without a fixed date. Later, the spring worship was set on the fifth Wu Day① after the Day of the Beginning of Spring, and the autumn worship is set on the fifth Wu Day after the Day of the Beginning of Autumn.

On Spring Earth Day, people offered sacrifices to the God of Earth and Grain for favorable

---

①The ancient people believe the five elements in the world are Water, Fire, Wood, Gold and Earth, which match the ten heavenly stems, such as Jia, Yi, Bing, Ding and Wu, where the Earth matches Wu, so it is called Wu day.Rites of Zhou, Thirteen Classics, Zhongzhou Ancient Books Publishing House,1992 weather, big harvest and good health. Besides, in this occasion, people have special food and drink and conduct other practices to celebrate. After Song and Yuan Dynasties, the date for spring worship was fixed on February 2nd of the lunar calendar, and people took the day as the birthday of the God of Earth. A variety of customs and practice of the previous Spring Earth Day were handed over to the Day of February 2nd. Therefore, February 2nd inherits the festival connotation of the Spring Earth Day, which values agriculture and farm work, and looks forward to favorable weather and a good harvest.

寿年丰的日子，同时还是一个有着特殊饮食和其他习俗的节日。宋元以后，春社日期逐渐固定在农历二月初二日。人们将二月二视为土地公公的生日，春社日的诸多节俗也移至二月二进行。二月二由此继承了社日重农务本、祈求风调雨顺、农业丰收的节日内涵。

4. The Zhonghe Festival

The Zhonghe Festival used to be celebrated on the first day of February, which was originally observed on Tang Dynasty under the rule of Emperor De (779—805). Zeng Zao in his Collection of Literary Sketches quoted from the Biography of the Marquis Ye's Family written by Li Fan described in details about the Day:

Emperor De said, "The previous regimes all have celebrations in the third nine-day period after the Winter Solstice; now Shangsi Festival often falls on the same day as the Cold Food Festival (the day

四、中和节

中和节节期在二月初一，是唐朝德宗时期始创的一个节日。这在曾慥《类说》引李繁《邺侯家传》"中和节"条中有详细的记述：

德宗曰："前代三九皆有公会，而上巳与寒食往往同时，来年合是三月二日寒食，乃春无公会矣。欲于二月创置一节，何日而可？"

泌曰："二月十五日以后虽是花时，与寒食相值，又近晦日，以晦为节，非佳名色。二月一日，正是桃李开时，请以二月一日为中和节。其日赐大臣方镇勋戚尺，谓之裁度。令人家以青囊盛百谷果实相间遗，谓之献生子。酝酒，谓之宜春酒。村间祭勾芒神，祈谷，百僚进农书，以示务本。"

上大悦，即令行之，并与上巳、重阳谓之三令节，中外皆赐钱，寻胜宴会。①

由上述记载可知，中和节首先是由唐德宗提

before Qingming Festival when only cold food is served), which is on March 2nd in the coming year. It seems that we have no festivals in spring. I would like to set up a festival in February, what do you think?"

Mi replied, "The flower blossoming time comes after February 25th, but it is too close to the Cold Food Festival and to the last day of a month, which is not an auspicious day of a festival. February 1st is often the time for peaches and plums blossoming, which is a good sign. I believe it is appropriate to name this day as the Zhonghe Festival. On that day, the emperor will reward ministers the peerage ruler representing the authority of making the right decision; Ordinary people will pack all kinds of fruits and grains in blue bags and give them away to each other as a way of sending gifts; the households will make wines for the coming of spring; villages will offer sacrifices to the God of Gou Mang (a mythological figure who is in charge of forestry and agriculture), praying for a good harvest; and all officials will hand in books of farm work to show their respect to agriculture."

The emperor was pleased and gave approval to this proposal. Therefore, the Day of Balance becomes one of the Three Festivals, together with the Day of Shangsi and the Double Ninth Festival. On this day, money was given to officials and citizens, and parties were held to celebrate.①

According to the history above, the Zhonghe Festival was first proposed by Emperor De; Li Mi

①[宋]曾慥编：《类说》，上海：上海古籍出版社，1993年，第873页。

① Edited by Zeng Zao of Song Dynasty, *Collections of Literature Sketches*, Shanghai Ancient Books Publishing House, 1993, p. 873.

designed the details of the celebration activities, which were also approved by the emperor. An imperial edict was promulgated as follows:

"To show respect to alternate seasons, every dynasty added new festivals to the traditional ones. Han Dynasty came up with the Shangsi Day, and Jin Dynasty established the Double Ninth Festival. Some may suggest removing the old customs, but as these are happy occasions for my people and a chance for me to share the joys with them, I believe they should be kept and celebrated. I, as the emperor, propose that we take the first day of the second month of the lunar calendar as the Day of Balance, as the early spring is coming with trees and grasses sprouting, which is a season for growing with the heaven and the earth in harmony and balance. Celebrations of this day would replace the previous festivities at the end of January and the day fits in all the traditional practice of holidays passed down to our generations. On this day, all officials take a day off for the celebrations." [1]

议，李泌作了详细设计，并得到皇帝首肯，遂在贞元五年（789年）正月颁布诏书如下：

"四序嘉辰，历代增置，汉崇上巳，晋纪重阳。或说禊除，虽因旧俗，与众共乐，咸合当时。朕以春方发生，候及仲月，勾萌毕达，天地同和，俾其昭苏，宜助畅茂。自今宜以二月一日为中和节，以代正月晦日，备三令节数，内外官司休假一日。" [1]

---

[1] Liu Xu of Later Jin Dynasty: *Tang Annals,* Chung Hwa Book Co., 1975, p367.

[1][后晋]刘昫：《旧唐书》，北京：中华书局，1975年，第367页。

2 节俗流变
A Change of Customs

纵观二月二的历史演变，其节俗流变大致可分为四个阶段：唐宋时期定型，元明时期转型，清代和民国时期达到兴盛，20世纪中期以来逐渐衰弱。

一、定型于唐宋

如前所述，中唐以后，二月二逐步成为一个具有稳定节俗的节日，踏青、挑菜、迎富是其主要节俗活动。宋时依然如此。在宋代文学作品中，"踏青""挑菜"两词屡屡出现。

The customs and practice of February 2nd have changed over time, which can be divided into four phases: it came into shape in Tang and Song Dynasties; and then went through various changes during Yuan and Ming Dynasties; it reached its heyday in Qing and the Republican period; and since the mid-20th century, it goes to a decline.

1.Tang and Song Dynasties: the Shaping Period

As is mentioned in previous chapters, February 2nd became a holiday with fixed festival practice since mid-Tang Dynasty, with spring outing, vegetable picking and the God of Wealth greeting as its main activities. In Song Dynasty, these customs remained almost the same. Words like "spring outing" and "vegetable picking" frequently appeared in literature works at that time.

In Song Dynasty, this vegetable-picking practice became popular even within the royal family, where it was called "vegetable picking dinner". It was more like a game to the royal members with a series of rules, including rewards and punishment, which was recorded in Zhou Mi's *Records on Urban Life*:

On the second day, a vegetable-picking dinner party will be held in the palace. A crucible decorated with red and green flowers was presented. Reels of cloth of silk were put inside it. On each reel of cloth of silk, names of vegetables were written, such as lettuce and caltrop. Red threads were tied to the reels of silk. After dinner when music was on, people lined up from the middle of the hall to its two sides and began to pick up those reels of silk in the container with a golden rod in hand. Concubines, princes and princesses all took part in this game and got rewarded without punishment. If the cloth of silk they picked up had vegetable name written in red on it, the picker would be rewarded, and if it was in black, there would be a punishment. The best prizes were pearls, jade cups, gold vessels, emeralds, combs, earrings, collar decorations, etc. Prizes for second place were silver, drinking vessels, bracelets, flowerlike jewelries, silks, ambergris, fans, pens and ink, and porcelains. The punishments were to entertain all royal guests present, including dancing and singing, reciting poems, chanting Buddhist sutras, drinking cold water, and eating ginger.

The game rewarded those who picked up the names of vegetables written in red and punished those who got the names written in black, which

宋时，挑菜之俗还传到宫中，演化为"挑菜御宴"，具有很强的游戏色彩。周密在《武林旧事》中详细描写了宫中挑菜游戏的做法和赏罚：

二日，宫中排办挑菜御宴。先是内苑预备朱绿花斛，下以罗帛作小卷，书品目于上，系以红丝，上植生菜、荠花诸品。俟宴酬乐作，自中殿以次，各以金篦挑之。后妃、皇子、贵主、婕妤及都知等，皆有赏无罚。以次每斛十号，五红字为赏，五黑字为罚。上赏则成号珍珠、玉杯、金器、北珠、篦环、珠翠、领抹，次亦铤银、酒器、冠镯、翠花、段帛、龙涎、御扇、笔墨、官窑、定器之类。罚则舞唱、吟诗、念佛、饮冷水、吃生姜之类，用此以资嬉笑。

皇宫中的这一游戏，对挑中红色书写的野菜名的人给予奖赏，对挑中黑色书写的野菜名的人进行惩罚，十分有趣，引得"王宫贵邸，亦多效之"。

总体看，唐宋时期的二月二是个充满快乐的节日，其社会活动主要是在户外进行踏青、挑菜和迎富等，体现着时人对大自然的亲近热爱以及对富足生活的期盼。

二、转型于元明

元明时期的二月二，在继承踏青、挑菜、迎富等习俗的同时，又增加了一些新的节俗活动，如撒灰之俗。值得注意的是，此时的二月二已与"龙抬头"一说联系起来。元末人士熊梦祥在《析津志·岁纪》中载："二月二日，谓之龙抬头。五更时，各家以石灰于井畔周遭糁引白道，直入家中房内，男子、妇人不用扫地，恐惊了龙眼睛。"到了明代，与龙、撒灰相关的习俗记载明显增多。比如沈榜《宛署杂记》第十七卷载"二月引龙"，并在注中进一步解释：

was so interesting that "many aristocratic families began to follow the practice".

Generally speaking, the Day of February 2nd in Tang and Song Dynasties was a festival full of fun; its major outdoor activities were spring outing, vegetable picking and Wealth God greeting, which showed people's love for nature and their expectations for an abundant life.

2. Yuan and Ming Dynasties: the Transitional Period

The Day of February 2nd in Yuan and Ming Dynasties saw an addition of new festival activities to the traditional spring greeting, vegetable picking and Wealth God greeting, such as ash spreading. It was worth noticing that the day then was already associated with the so-called "dragon raising head". In *Annals of Xijin*, Xiong Mengxiang of the late Yuan Dynasty wrote, "February 2nd is called the Day of Dragon Head Raising. Between three to five o'clock in the morning, all households will spread lime around the wells; no sweeping of the floor is allowed in case the dragon will hurt in the eyes." In Ming Dynasty, records on the custom related to dragons and ash spreading were evidently increasing. For instance, in Shen Bang's *Notes By the Officer of Wan*, the seventeenth chapter was "Calling for the Dragons in February", and in annotation, the author wrote, "People in Wan County called February 2nd as the Day of Dragon Head Raising. People in countryside would spread the ash slowly from outside to the sitting room and the kitchen, around the water vat; this is the practice of calling for the dragons."

During this period, festival customs such as smoking away the insects, married women visiting their parents and grain barn filling were already observed in common people's life.

Demonstrated by the above historical records, major customs of February 2nd such as calling for dragons, spreading ash, grain barn filling, smoking insects, and greeting the married daughters all appeared in Yuan and Ming Dynasties, which greatly changed the nature of the Day, and transformed the festival from a simple, entertaining holiday into a composite type of holiday with rich connotations and colorful customs such as worshipping the dragons and the earth, keeping away from pests, and praying for health and harvest.

3. The Qing Dynasty and the Republic of China: the Prime Period

February 2nd in Qing Dynasty and the Republic of China inherited the previous customs and festival activities and practice mentioned above, and more rituals were derived from the original customs such as worshiping the dragons and the earth, keeping away from pests, and praying for health and harvest, which makes the festival popular in a wider range. According to *Local Chronicles in China: Information Compilation on Folk Customs*,

"宛人呼二月二为龙抬头。乡民用灰自门外委婉布入宅厨，旋绕水缸，呼为引龙回。"

这一时期，熏虫、嫁女归宁、填仓等节俗在民间社会也已出现。

可见，二月二的重要节俗如引龙、撒灰、填仓、驱虫、迎女等，在元明时期都已出现，二月二原有的节日性质也因此而大大改变，从一个内容相对单调、娱乐色彩浓厚的节日转化成为一个内涵十分丰富，以崇龙祀土、驱避害虫、祈求人寿年丰为核心内容的复合型节日。

三、兴盛于清朝和民国

清朝和民国时期的二月二，继承了前人二月二的主要节俗活动，并围绕着崇龙祀土、驱避害虫、祈求人寿年丰等核心内涵衍生出更多仪式，使二月二节俗内容更加丰富多彩，流传地域更加广泛。丁世良、赵放主编的《中国地方志民俗资料汇编》一书，将明清以来，尤其是清朝以来各个时期编修的地方志中的民俗资料汇集成册，从中可以详细地了解二月二的节俗活动及其在全国各地的流布情况。我们看到这一时期二月二的流传地域很广，全国30多个省级行政区划，除新疆、西藏和青海以外，其余均有关于二月二节俗的记载。这段时期的二月二节俗，包括撒灰、祀神、占卜、迎女、剃头、踏青、迎富、击房梁炕沿、照虫烛、制作驱虫物品、戴龙尾、试耕、种菜、饭牛、吃犒劳酒、开笔取兆、上坟等，并形成了特定的节日饮食和节日饰品，此外还有很多关于二月二的禁忌。显然，二月二在清朝和民国时期已进入兴盛期。

edited by Ding Shiliang and Zhao Fang, which has collected information on folk customs in various regions in China since Qing Dynasty, the customs of February 2nd were widely spread. Among over 30 provincial administration divisions, except Xinjiang, Qinghai and Tibet, all of the rest provinces have records on the celebrations of February 2nd. Festival practice during this period included ash spreading, god worshipping, divination, married daughter greeting, haircut, spring outing, Wealth God greeting, beam striking, insects candling and expelling, wearing "dargon's tail", ploughing, growing vegetables, feeding cows, having dinners, teaching children to write, and visiting graves of the died family members. The colorful customs indicate that the Day of February 2nd reached its heyday in this period.

4.Modern Time: the Declining Period

Since 1950s, the Day of February 2nd began to phase out of people's life as a festival, with a variety of celebrating activities fading away, such as the calling for dragons, barn filling, insects expelling and earth worshipping; certain rituals and taboos are not observed any more. While aged people still keep the old day's traditions in their mind, most of the young people pay little attention to the rituals and activities. This time-honored agricultural festival now only leaves a faint print on modern life as all the young generation can remember about the day is the old saying of "dragon head raising" and eating frying green beans. The Day of February 2nd is running the risk of being lost in time.

The Day of February 2nd is not alone in this trend which culture traditional is facing the dilemma. Traditional culture as a whole is faced with such dangers in modern society. In the contemporary history of China, traditional culture has always been placed in an awkward position; it is desolated, neglected and even criticized. "Since China started its modernization in late Qing Dynasty, there have always been disagreements between traditional and modern way of life. At a time when authorities and intellectuals all believed that only by breaking out of the old can they set up new rules, and only by

四、近现代的衰落

20世纪中叶以来，二月二进入衰落期。其最明显的标志是，许多节俗活动逐渐淡出人们的日常生活，引龙、围仓、驱虫、祀土地等都已不再常见，相关禁忌也较少被遵循。就传承主体而言，除了老年人群体对二月二还念念不忘之外，绝大多数年轻人已不再注重相应的仪式和行为。一个几千年来具有农耕意义的传统节日，留给当代年轻人的似乎只剩下关于"龙抬头"的说法以及吃炒豆等模糊的记忆碎片，二月二节俗传承出现断裂。

这种状况的出现，其实与传统文化在现代社会中的整体性境遇相关。在中国近现代历史上，传统文化处境尴尬，常被视作阻碍历史车轮滚滚向前的旧文化的一部分，在不同程度上受到冷落、轻视甚至批判。"自清朝后期中国开始现代化进程以来，就一直存在着传统和现代的争执。曾几何时，无论官方还是众多知识精英，都以为只有破旧才能立新，只有抛弃传统才能走向现代，于是包括传统节日在内的传统文化一律被视为落后的、封建的而受到抨击和排斥。"①特别是在20世纪上半叶的中国社会，革命化、西方化的势头一浪高过一浪，广大农民常被视为愚夫愚妇，成为被重点改造的对象。与之相应的是，农耕文化逐步被边缘化，与民众生产生活密切相关的传统节日厄运难逃，被视作一种落后的、愚昧的、需要革除的文化予以多方取缔，其生存空间逐步被压缩，传统节日的传承危机概由此生。

1949年新中国成立，国家政府曾给予传统节日一定的地位，如将农历正月初一称作"春节"，并规定春节放假三天。然而，新成立的国家政权急需对国民进行思想

discarding the tradition can they build a modern China, the traditional cultures including traditional festivals were considered so outdated and feudal that they must be criticized and repelled." Especially in the first fifty years in China, the trend of revolution and westernization was growing rapidly. Farmers were considered as fatuous illiterates to be enlightened and transformed, and thus agricultural culture was marginalized. Traditional festivals related to farm work were also regarded as outdated and benighted which needed to be reformed and even be forbidden. Traditional festivals are losing their battles against the modern trend and thus the crisis begins.

When People's Republic of China was founded in 1949, the new government once resumed the position of certain festivals. For example, the first day of the New Year in lunar calendar was named "Spring Festival" and given three-day holidays to celebrate the day. However, when the newly founded reign started its reform on people's idea by attacking

①张勃：《从传统到当下：试论官方对传统节日的干预》，《民俗研究》2005年第1期。

①Zhang Bo: *From the Past to the Present: A Probe into the Official Intervention in Traditional Festival Celebration, Folklore Studies*,2005(1)

the Four Olds (old customs, old habits, old ideas and old concepts) and setting up the Four News (new customs, new habits, new ideas and new concepts), traditional connotations of these festivals were replaced and distorted. In the following "Cultural Revolution", common people were forced to stop celebrating traditional festivals or their lives would be threatened. Fortunately, the Reform and Opening Up period brought back the life of these traditional festivals; they receive great attention and become popular again in people's daily life.

As for the Day of February 2nd, some celebrating activities and practice are recovered and maintained, such as drawing the granary on the ground and enclosing the grain barn, which is still very popular in the southwest of Shandong Province; festival foods such as fried beans, millet flour pancakes and spring pancakes can be found in various occasions; temple fairs on the Day of February 2nd to worship dragon kings and God of Earth are also prevailing; and it becomes common practice for people to wash and cut their hairs on that day all over the country. In some places, a variety of new practice are observed to celebrate the day. In conclusion, the Day of February 2nd is adapted to the modern society with its strong vitality and turning into new shapes while reserving its old traditions.

改造，"破四旧"（旧风俗、旧习惯、旧思想、旧观念）、"立四新"（新风俗、新习惯、新思想、新观念）蔚然成风。在此背景下，传统节日内容被予以"革命化"的置换，变得面目全非。随之而来的"文化大革命"，更是强迫普通民众疏离传统节俗活动，否则就会遭罹祸端。改革开放以来，我国兴起"民俗热"，传统节日进入复兴期，越来越受到国人的重视。

具体到二月二而言，其部分节俗活动得到恢复和存留，比如打囤、囤仓目前在鲁西南地区仍然普遍流行；炒蝎豆、摊煎饼、吃春饼等食俗也时有所见。而以龙王、土地等神为祭祀对象的二月二庙会在不少地方依然盛行，二月二洗头理发的做法更是风行全国。在某些地区，二月二期间许多新的节俗活动悄然兴起。二月二正以其顽强的生命力去适应当代社会的种种需求，并在传承旧节俗的同时发生着新的蜕变。

3 二月二的流布
Geographical Variation

作为一个历史悠久的传统节日，二月二在全国各地广为流传。据《中国地方志民俗资料汇编》《中国民间文学集成》等资料判断，二月二在除西藏自治区以外的全国33个省、市、自治区均有流传，其范围之广，堪比春节、清明、端午、中秋等四大传统节日。这主要是因为，中国是个农业大国，而二月二是春耕开始的标志，与农事活动密切关联，故在我国传统的农耕社会中占有重要地位。以祭祀土地神为例，除宁

As a time-honored traditional festival, the Day of February 2nd is widely spread throughout the country. According to *Local Chronicles in China: Information Compilation on Folk Customs* and *Collections of Chinese Folk Literature*, except Tibet, all of the 33 provincial and municipal administration divisions celebrate the Day of February 2nd, making it one of the most popular traditional holidays like Spring Festival, Tomb-Sweeping Day, Dragon Boat Festival and Mid-Autumn Festival. China is an agricultural country and February 2nd is closely related to agricultural activities as it marks the beginning of a year's farm work, therefore, the Day becomes so important in our traditional agrarian society. For example, the practice of worshipping the God of Earth on February 2nd is observed all over the country except in Ningxia, Tibet and Yunnan[1].

The Day of February 2nd is a festival for the Han nationality, which is the reason why in ethnic minorities residences, it is celebrated only by Han people; all of the records on this day is written in Han's language. Narrations of the Day among ethnic minorities can rarely be seen, but according to materials and information at hand, some minorities also celebrate the day, such as Zhuang people in Lianshan County, Guangdong Province, Tujia people in Xiangxi Autonomous District, Hunan Province, She people in Fuding County, Fujian Province, Yi people in Yunnan Province and Miao people[2] in Guizhou Province. Tujia people in Xiangxi, Hunan take the day as the birthday of the God of Earth, and they would offer the pig head as sacrifices to the god according to local folk proverbs. She people in Shuanghua Village of Qianqi in Fuding County, Fujian, have their own legend of the origin of the day that is different from the Han people's version. According to local proverbs from Azhe

---

[1]Han People in Yunnan worship the God of Dragon, instead of God of Earth on February 2nd. On this day, soldiers and civilians all offer sacrifices to the gods, and the government officials attend the worship ceremony, the banquet as well as the opera performances. For the first three days, there is a worshipping ceremony in the army camp and another ceremony in Black Dragon Lake on the next day. Ceremonies in other places all start on the second day. Local people conduct the ceremony in their own ways. It is cited from *Records of Yimen County Revised in the Reign of Daoguang, Qing Dynasty*, volume 7: Folk Customs, revised by Yan Tingyü, compiled by Yan Zhongze.
[2]Wang PingLi:*Bridge-worshipping Day of Miao People in Southeast of Guizhou, Heilongjiang National Series*(quarterly edition), 1999, volume 4.

夏、西藏、云南[1]外，全国其他地区都有关于二月二祭祀土地神的记载。

从民族的角度看，二月二主要是汉族的传统节日，比如在宁夏、新疆、云南等少数民族聚居区，就主要是汉族时兴过二月二节，与二月二有关的文献记载基本上都是汉族的。少数民族有关二月二的记述较少，就目前资料来看，广东连山县的壮族、湖南湘西自治州的土家族、福建福鼎县的畲族、云南的彝族、贵州的苗族[2]等都有过二月二的习俗。如湖南湘西土家族以二月初二日为土地生日，要以猪头祭祀，当地有"二月二，龙抬头，土地堂前许猪头"之谚。在福建福鼎县前岐乡双华村的畲族聚居区，

---

[1]云南地区的汉族在二月二主要祭祀龙神，而非土地神。"二月二日，军民备牲醴，官诣大龙泉祭祀，宴会，演剧。初三日，安宁所屯军祭。次日，乌龙潭祭。其他各处龙泉俱于初二日祭。土人自为之祭之。"见（清）严廷珏修、严仲泽纂：《清道光续修易门县志》（卷七·风俗志）。
[2]王萍丽：《黔东南苗族二月初二敬桥节》，《黑龙江民族丛刊》1999年第4期。

流传着"'二月二'的由来"的传说。在云南省红河地区彝族阿哲支系，要在正月初二这天送火神上天，保佑来年平安不遭火灾，而在二月初二这天祭龙神，则有"正月间，送火星；二月二，祭龙日"之谚。

从二月二节俗活动上看，受地理因素、民族因素影响较大，南北地区差异明显，各区域族群间不尽相同。从地理方位上说，大致可将二月二流行地区划分为以下五大板块：①东北、华北和西北局部地区，包括东北三省、北京、天津、河北、山东、河南、山西、陕西、甘肃等。这一地区的二月二节日活动较为隆重，主要节日习俗保存相对完整，如引龙、撒灰、围仓、嫁女归宁、剃头等；在节日饮食上有炒豆、吃年糕、水饺、面条（龙须）等，体现出麦作文化的特征。同时，该地区多有在二月二这天举办庙会的情景。②华东地区，包括江苏、上海、浙江、

tribe of Yi people in Yunnan, people should see off the God of Fire to the heaven on that day so as to bless a good year without fire disasters, and also offer sacrifices to the God of Dragon.

Celebrating activities of February 2nd vary between north and south regions and among nationalities, influenced by geographic factors and national differences. Geographically, regions and places that celebrate the day can be divided into five parts: (1) Northeast China, North China and Northwest China, including the three provinces in Northeast (Heilongjiang, Liaoning and Jilin), Beijing, Tianjin, Hebei, Shandong, Henan, Shanxi, Shaanxi and Gansu. Activities there are solemn and well-preserved, such as calling for dragons, spreading ash, enclosing the barn, greeting married daughters and haircut. Festival foods include frying beans, rice cake, dumplings and noodles (like dragon's beard), all reflecting the wheat agricultural culture. People in the regions also hold temple fairs on the Day of February 2nd for celebration. (2) East China, including Jiangsu, Shanghai, Zhejiang, Fujian and Jiangxi. The Day of February 2nd in these areas was called "Flowering Day" in ancient times, and spring outing and spring parties were very popular then. Festival foods include rice with leaf mustard and rice cake, which are very distinct under the rice agriculture. (3) Central China and

Southwest China, including Anhui, Hubei, Hunan, Chongqing, Sichuan and Guizhou. Customs and festival foods in those regions combine the features of both wheat-related and rice-related agriculture. (4) South China, including Guangdong, Guangxi, Hainan, Hong Kong, Taiwan and Macao. Customs of February 2nd focus on the worship of the God of Earth, and a variety of new forms of celebration are added in its evolvement and merged with local festivals. For example, there is Self-selling Festival in Dongguan, Guangdong Province, and Cannon Festival in Yangchun. (5) Other regions, including Yunnan, Ningxia, Inner Mongolia, Qinghai and Xinjiang, most of which are ethnic minorities residences, where only the residents of Han people celebrate the Day of February 2nd. The celebrating practice is greatly influenced by local ethnic minorities and, therefore, quite different from those in other regions. For instance, Han people in Yunnan Province will hold some rites to offer sacrifices to dragon, "On the Day of February 2nd, the villager

福建、江西等。在这一地区，古时又将二月二称为"花朝节"，曾广泛流行踏青、宴饮之俗，在节日饮食方面时兴制作芥菜饭、炒粿箸、撑腰糕等，具有稻作文化的特征。③华中和西南局部地区，包括安徽、湖北、湖南、重庆、四川、贵州等，这一地区的二月二兼具麦作文化和稻作文化的特征。④华南地区，包括广东、广西、海南、港澳台等。这一地区的二月二节俗以祭祀土地神为核心，在后世的发展中又与当地一些节庆活动融合，出现了一些新的形式，如广东东莞的"卖身节"、阳春市的"梁镇南将军府炮会"等。⑤其他地区，包括云南、宁夏、内蒙古、青海、新疆等，属于少数民族聚居区域，居住于该地区的汉族人有过二月二之俗，但其节俗明显受到当地少数民族的影响而与其他地区大异其趣。如云南汉族多在二月二这天举行祭龙仪式："二月二日，乡村祭龙。"① "二月二日于龙潭祭龙修禊，用灶灰撒墙根，以却虫虺。养蚕之家，于惊蛰日晒蚕种。"②在宁夏地区，二月二被看作一个团圆的节日，"二月二日，将元旦所做炉饼集老幼于庭食之，名'团圆饼'，取一年团圆之意"③。

all go to worship the dragons."[1] "On the second day of February, people go to Dragon Pond to worship the dragons, and spread kitchen ash along walls in their houses to get rid of insects; families that feed the silkworms all move the cocoons into the open air for sunshine on the Day of Insects Waking."[2] In Ningxia, February 2nd is considered as a day for reunion. "On the second day of February, people would take out the cakes made on the first day of the New Year and eat together with family members, old and young. The cake is called reunion cake, indicating people's hope for a happy reunion of the family."[3]

①[民国]朱文锦纂，云南学会编：《民国云南省地志》，1921年，第24页

②（清）黎洵修，刘荣黼纂：《清道光大姚县志》（卷之二：地理志下），参见：杨成彪主编：《楚雄彝族自治州旧方志全书》，昆明：云南出版社，2005年，第110页。

③马福祥、陈必淮修，王之臣纂：《灵州新志》，天津华泰书局铅印本，民国十六年。

①Compiled by Zhu Wenjin of the Republic of China, edited by Yunnan Academic Society, *Chorography of Yunnan in the Republic of China*, 1921, p.24.

②Compiled by Li Xun and by Liu Rongfu of Qing Dynasty, *Records of Dayao County in the Reign of Daoguang of Qing Dynasty* (volume 2: geography part two), which is referred in *Old Records of Autonomous Region of Yi People in Chuxiong*(Dayao volume, part one), edited by Yang Chengbiao, Kunming: Yunnan Publishing House, 2005, p.110.

③revied by Ma Fuxiang and Chen Bihuai, compiled by Wang Zhicheng, *New Record of Linzhou*, Stereotype edition by Tianjin Huatai Publishing House, 1927.

第二章 二月二的风俗

　　二月二节俗起源于唐代，此后根据二月的气候、物候、月令、宜忌等，历朝历代经过不断调整完善，吸纳了惊蛰、春社等节俗活动，节日内容逐渐丰富。从节日的行为规范来看，二月二对于那些从蛰伏状态下重生和复活的自然界生灵给予关注，尤其对虫、龙等特别关注。人们通过一系列带有巫术性质的习俗活动，对这些生灵与人类之间相生相克的关系予以神秘化、神圣化，希望借助想象这些自然生灵力量加以调控和调动，重新建构起它们与人类的关系，以改善人们的生活质量，提升劳动者的身体能量，祈求人寿年丰、风调雨顺。

Chapter Two

Customs of February 2nd

Customs of February 2nd started in Tang Dynasty and was adjusted according to the climate, the biotemperature, the phenology and Feng Shui in February, taking in cultural activities from other festivals such as the Day of Insects Waking and Spring Earth Day to enrich the celebrating activities on that day. It becomes one of the main themes of the Day that creatures of the great nature are revived from hibernation, which draws people's imagination to the insects and dragons. A series of festival practice related to witchcraft were adopted to mystify and sanctify the relationship of mutually reinforcing and neutralizing each other between these creatures and mankind; it is hoped that by borrowing and balancing the forces of creatures, people are able to rebuild the relationship between themselves, improve their life qualities and promote their physical power; and the new year will come with a good harvest, a healthy body and favorable weather.

1 祈福纳祥
Pray

Agriculture is the foundation of the traditional Chinese society, and farming industry weigh heavily on national economy and are closely related to people's livelihood. The Day of February 2nd falls on the second month of spring when the earth is waking up from the winter sleep and spring farm work is about to begin, therefore, its festival customs are concerned with the agricultural activities. Rainfalls are most needed in this season, especially in North China. Dragons are considered as the god in charge of the rain, who always stay under water in seclusion during autumn and winter and won't come out until spring is on its way. February 2nd is the day for dragons to "raise their heads" and come out of the water, thus a great many activities on that day all have something to do with dragons, of which "inviting the dragons" is the most special one.

中国传统社会，历来以农业为立国之本，农业生产的丰歉直接关系着国计民生。二月二时处仲春，是春回大地、万物复苏、春耕生产即将全面开始的季节，其节俗活动自然与农业生产有莫大关系。春耕时节最需要的就是雨水，在春雨贵如油的北方地区尤其如此。在民众的心目中，龙是司雨之神，秋冬之间往往潜入水中蛰伏不出，直到春天才会重新醒来。二月二正是"龙抬头"的日子，这天有不少活动便是围绕龙而进行的。其中，最富特色的要数"引龙"了。

一、引龙

引龙，也称"领龙""引钱龙""引龙迦""引龙填仓"等，是我国北方地区二月二期间常见的节俗。所谓引龙，就是人们将灶灰或谷糠撒在地上，蜿蜒成龙形，将"龙"小心翼翼地引回家中。引龙的目的是驱除虫害，招福纳祥。俗信龙总是居于水中，因此引龙的起点往往是河、井等处，而终点则是家中的水缸。各地引龙方式不尽相同，有的把灰从大门外蜿蜒撒入厨房，然后围水缸一周；也有的用糠撒到井里，再用灰撒线由井水处直入家室。在辽宁本溪地区，二月二这天一大早，当家人便要洗漱干净，穿戴整齐，用铁锹在灶坑里扒些新备小灰，装在篮子里，拿着铁锹，挎着篮子来到井边或河边去领龙。当地领得越早，过得越好，所以天刚亮的时候人们便争相去领龙。领龙时，以锹撒灰，

1.Inviting Dragons

Inviting Dragons, also named "bringing in the dragons" or "bringing in forture dragons and filling the barns", is a common festival practice in North China on February 2nd. To invite dragons is to spread the kitchen ash or grain chaffs on the ground to make the shape of dragon and carefully lead it into your house. The aim is to get rid of pests and to bring good luck and fortune to the family. It is believed that dragons live in the waters, so the trip of "inviting dragon" often starts from the river bank or near the well and ends in the water vat of the house. The ways to attract the dragons home vary in different places. In some areas, traces of ash winding into the house from outside the door would then circle around the water vat; in other places, the grain chaffs are spread into the well and lead directly into the house by strings covered with ash. In Benxi,

Liaoning Province, early in the morning of February 2nd, the whole family would firstly clean and well-dress themselves, then collect the newly burnt ash from the hearth with a small spade; the ash is carried in a basket to the river bank or near the well to attract dragons. It is believed that the collection of ash should be done as early as possible on that day, therefore, people all get up before the sunrise to scramble for a better chance. When inviting the dragons, the small spade is used to spread the ash into a shape of dragon, which should be a curve, the thinner the better. The curve of ash will reach to the water vat, the hearth and the barns of the house, which means the dragon is invited into the house. Later, the family will connect the curve of ash with more ash, drawing circles of the similar sizes in the courtyard, each with a cross-shaped drawing in it, which symbolizes the barn; then wheat, rice and corns will be put into each circle separately, and livestocks such as chicken and ducks will be let out and led to these circles; it is said that the first sort of grain to be eaten up by these animals will have the highest output in the coming year. Some families will draw a ladder by lines of ash between the circles and the door of the house, which means that the dragons in heaven can find their way to the house. In Yuncheng and Linqu, Shandong Province, people will spread ash (from the burnt grass and trees) around the house to keep away the pangolin, a kind of animal that can dig the hole to water in the house, which is said to be able to hold back the flood.

灰线撒得越细越好，要呈弯曲状，一直撒到自家的水缸、灶台及仓房处，以示将龙领回。随后，当家人用小灰接继领龙时的灰线，在院中撒成大小一致的多个圆圈，并在圆圈内画上十字，以示粮囤，再将麦子、谷子、苞米等杂粮撒在每个"粮囤"内，将鸡、鸭等家畜放出，看家畜先吃掉哪种粮食，就预示来年哪种粮食会丰收。有的人家还在要"粮囤"与自家房屋的门口处，画些梯子状的灰线，以求"飞龙上天"，将龙领进家内。在山东郓城、临朐一带还在房子周围撒一圈草木灰，称之"打围墙"，据说可以防止"领水之兽"穿山甲进宅子，以此阻挡洪水。

二、剃龙头

全国各地普遍时兴二月二理发，谓之"剃龙头"。民间俗信，不出正月不能剃头，否则被认为对舅舅有妨，即所谓"正月不剃头，剃头死舅舅"。出了正月，头发已经蓄长，倘若这天洗头或是剪头发，顿有头清目爽之感。又因二月二是"龙抬头"的日子，人们取其寓意吉祥，这天理发即意味着未来一年内都会发丝黑壮、聪明伶俐。每到二

2.Shaving Dragon's Head

It is a common nationwide practice to have a haircut on February 2nd, which is called "shaving dragon's head". People believe that it is improper to cut hair during January, as there was a saying that "Dont's have a hairunt in January, or your uncle must meet a disaster, even death." Therefore, when January is over, everyone wears long beard and hair, and a refreshing haircut is greatly in need. People choose to cut their hair on February 2nd as it is the day when "dragons raise their heads", which sounds auspicious and lucky. They hope that when they have a haircut on that very day, they will look smart and have a clever mind for a whole year. That's why the barbers, are always crowded on that day.

Traditionally, the haircut on February 2nd is done by the elders in the family or by family friends. Often anyone who is bold enough can cut hair for others. Boys are often asked to shave all hair off the head, which is a painful experience clearly remembered by our grandfathers till today. On the early morning of February 2nd, children were asked to wash their heads in the river or ditches near the road. After that, the head shaving began. As it was painful to have a knife to shave the hair off, most boys were reluctant to have the haircut; therefore, adults of the family had to force the boy to take part in this ritual activity or even tied him up in case that his naughty struggles would interrupt the ritual activity or hurt himself. Today, as life is much better than the old days, most people go to the barber's to have a haircut on February 2nd, but some old

月二，城乡理发店常常人满为患。

在传统社会，二月二剪头发常常是由家里的长辈或亲戚朋友来完成。通常，无论男女，只要胆子稍大，敢于下手的人都可以给别人剪头发。而且，男孩子通常是要剃光头的，这可是件痛苦的事。至今，许多老人对那段痛苦的经历还记忆犹新。二月二一大早，大人便会让小孩到河里或者有积水的地沟去洗头。洗完了，便蹲在地上开始剃头。剃刀刮头是很疼的，小孩子怕疼不愿意理，大人便硬按着，有的小孩还被绑得不能动弹，怕剃不好，也怕

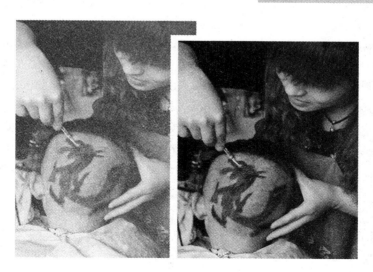

刮破头流血。如今，随着生活条件的改善，尽管很多地区还沿袭着"二月二，剪龙头"的习俗，但除少数老年人还在家中自己剪头发以外，多数人都会到理发店中打理。对于他们来说，二月二理发固然是在遵从传统习俗，但所理发型及头发长短，是关系到脸面和时尚的问题。

三、祭祀龙王

二月二是"龙抬头"的日子，山西、山东、陕西、河南、广东等许多地方还有二月二祭龙王的习俗。在山西马邑，人们在这天祭献龙王，并在龙王庙附近聚餐，叫做"开庙会"。陕西米脂的农民也在这天会集于龙神庙，杀羊祭祀，叫作"开庙门"。河南林县不仅要祭龙神，还要祭碾碓，因为当地人认为碾碓都是属龙的。山东郓城也有类似的习俗，届时家家户户要把石磨的上扇支起，谓之"龙抬头"。俗说此举能使得"细雨下得满地流，

people still cut their hair at home to maintain the old practice of "shaving head on the day of Dragon Raising Head". For the young people today, they'd love to follow the tradition of having a haircut on the very day of February 2nd, but after all, the length of hair and hairstyles will have an important impast on their face and fashion in modern times.

3. Worshipping the Dragon King

In provinces like Shanxi, Shandong, Shaanxi and Henan, people observe the practice of worshipping the Dragon King on the Day of February 2nd. In Mayi County, Shanxi Province, people offer sacrifice to the Dragon King on that day and dine together near the Temple of Dragon King, which is called "temple fair gathering". Farmers in Mizhi County, Shaanxi Province, gather at the Dragon God Temple on that day and kill a goat as a sacrifice to the dragon god, which is called "opening the temple gate". In Lin County, Henan Province, people worship not only the dragon god, but also the grind and pestle, which is believed to be closely related to dragons. Similar customs can be found in Yuncheng, Shandong, where every household put up the upper part of the stone mill, indicating the so-called "dragon raising its head", which will bring "an in-time spring drizzle and ample food and

clothing for a whole year". In Qüfu, dragon lanterns are very popular on February 2nd. People go to the Temple of Dragon King in the southeast of the town to fetch waters and hold worship ceremony. Workers carrying water for Confucius Mansion are given some incenses and papers to burn near the well of drinking water outside the south gate of the Mansion as a worship ritual.

In Fanzhuang of Zhao County, Hebei, there is a grand ceremony called "Dragon Tablet Club". Members of the club worship the Dragon Tablet, which is usually enshrined in the house of the head of the Club. The head of the Club offers incenses and sacrifice every day to the tablet; on the first day and the fifteenth day of every month, people from the village or other villages will come to burn incense and make a wish to the tablet. The Club ceremony begins on the first day of February and ends at the fourth day. During the four days, a special tent will be set up for the dragon god;

一年吃穿不用愁"。在曲阜一带，二月二节俗期间时兴玩龙灯，此前一天到城东南的龙王庙取水，举行祭礼仪式。给孔府挑水的水夫，这天要领一封香、一表纸，到南门外拉甜水的井旁焚纸烧香。

在河北赵县范庄，二月二有规模盛大的"龙牌会"。龙牌会崇拜的是龙牌，俗称"龙牌爷"。龙牌平时供奉在会头家，会头负责每天上香上供，每逢初一、十五会有本村或外村的人前来烧香许愿。龙牌会自二月初一开始，初四结束，会期长达四天。届时，要搭建专门的龙棚，称为"醮棚"，延请道士举行打醮仪式，并将龙牌用黄幔大轿请到醮棚里，供人祭拜。龙牌会期间，要唱大戏，闹社火，家家户户邀朋会友、请亲待客。二月二是当地一年中最重大、最热闹的节日，比起过年、闹元宵也毫不逊色。

四、祭祀土地神

土地神即社神，民间也称土地爷、土地公公等。对土地神的祭祀遍布全国各地，但不同时代、不同地方祭祀的日期不一。明代以来，我国天津、山东、山西、江苏、上海、浙江、安徽、湖北、台湾、新疆、广东等区划内的不少地方都选择在二月二这天祭祀土地神。

过去祭祀土地神的仪式较为隆重，二月二日的"土地会"成为许多地区的一个重要节日。

在湖北大别山区，人们也在二月二作"土地会"。过去十几家为一社，"主东"带领民众在土地庙祭神，祈求消

it is called "religious tent", where Taoist priests are called in to hold religious rituals, and the Dragon Tablet is carried to the tent in a yellow-curtained sedan for worshipping. During this period, performances of operas and carnivals will be given; families invite friends and relatives to get together. It is one of the most significant and hilarious festivals in local community, no less than the Spring Festival and the Lantern Festival.

4. Worshipping the God of Earth

The God of Earth is called the Lord of Earth or Earth Grandfather in folk talks, the worship of which is prevailing all over the country, but the worshipping dates vary from different times and regions. Since Ming Dynasty, places in Tianjin, Shandong, Shanxi, Jiangsu, Shanghai, Zhejiang, Anhui, Hubei, Taiwan, Xinjiang and Guangdong all choose to worship the Earth God on February 2nd.

The ritual to worship the God of Earth was solemn and ceremonious in the past as Earth Ceremony became one of the major festivals in a variety of regions.

In Dabie Mountain area, Hubei Province, people also take part in the "Earth Ceremony" on February 2nd. In the past, a group of a dozen of households, led by one of the respected, would worship the god together in Earth Temple; they pray for the removal of illness, bringing fortune and the blessing from the heaven, prospering the livestock and health and peace for the family members. The host of the worship would invite people to dinner in his house after the ceremony, where they talked over wine about the farm work.

In Zhejiang, worshipping of Earth God on February 2nd is also a prevailing practice to celebrate the festival. According to *Official Chronicles of HangZhou*, it is in a local proverb that people have pan-fry cake and frying beans on February 2nd as a way to worship the earth. In Jiaxing, according to *Chronicles of Tongxiang County*, "On the second day of February, people wear leaves of bitter fleabane to prevent headache." In Huzhou region, according to *Chronicles of Gui'an County*, "On February 2nd, people worship the Earth God and wear leaves of bitter fleabane to prevent headache, as a proverb says, the fleabanes blossom before other plants, wearing whose leaves keep you forever young." In *Chronicles of Anji County*, "February 2nd is considered to be the birthday of the Earth God; the practice that neighbors gathered to drink on that day is called Earth Celebration." In She ethnic minority residence of Zhejiang Province, people also offer sacrifice to gods such as the Lord of Earth and pray for a better life, as a proverb goes, "On February 2nd, chickens are killed to sacrifice to the earth."

People in Guangdong also take February 2nd as the birthday for Grandpa Earth, which is called

灾赐福，福星高照，六畜兴旺，人丁平安。祭祀完毕，在主东家设宴，大家边饮酒边畅谈农事。

在浙江地区，二月二祭土地神是普遍存在的节俗活动。据《杭州府志》记载："'煎糕、炒豆'，杭之谚也。二月二日，以祀土地。"在嘉兴一带，据《桐乡县志》记载："二月二日，祀土地神，人戴蓬草以辟头风。"在湖州地区，据《归安县志》记载："二月初二日，祀土地神，士女皆摘蓬叶簪于首，曰辟头风。谚云'蓬开先百草，戴了春不老'。"在《安吉县志》中，也记载了"俗以为是日为'土地神诞'，里人酿视聚饮，曰'土地会'"。在浙江畲族地区，每年农历二月二人们备祭品祭祀土地爷等神，以保佑乡人平安，故当地有俗语谓"二月二，杀鸡请土地"。

旧时广东地区以农历二月初二为土地公公

诞辰，是日致祭，称为"土地诞"，俗称"伯公诞"，又叫社日。在祭拜社神时，人们往往结合着"打小人"之俗。平时或有噩梦，或遭小人暗算谗言，即去拜社神，并念叨"小人口舌，远赐他方。贵人扶持，小人远避"。拜社仪式一般由族中长老或村中较有威望的人主持，祭以猪头、三鸟（鸡、鸭、鹅）等，祭后以猪血猪杂做粥，名为"社粥"，与"社肉"一起分给乡民食用。

时至现代，民间祭祀土地爷的仪式一般都趋于简化。土地爷是一尊小神，庙宇极为简单，不受重视，俗云"土地老爷本姓张，有钱住大屋，没钱顶破缸"。民间又有"土地老爷担不起大供养"之说，四片瓦砾或一口破缸，覆在地上即可充当土地庙。然而，土地爷毕竟掌管一方土地，在它二月二生日之时不免要祭祀一番。俗话说"土地老爷也有个二月二"，说的就是这个道理。

Earth Day officially. When worshipping the Earth God, there is a practice of "cursing the bad guy"; if the prayer has nightmares or has been plotted in secret by a bad guy, he would be chanting, "Driving the bad guy away with his vicious tongue, the powerful and chiralrous man comes to help me so the bad guy has no guts to offend me any more", when worshipping the God of Earth. The worship ceremony is often hosted by the most respected villager or a senior villager; pig's head, chickens, ducks and gooses are presented as sacrifice to the god; after the ceremony, the rest of the pig and its blood are used to cook the porridge, "the porridge of Earth", which will be shared among the villagers with "the meat of Earth".

In modern times, the ceremony to worship the God of Earth is simplified. Earth God is a minor god whose temple is by no means a grand one. A proverb goes like this, "The Lord of Earth has a family name of Zhang, who lives in a worn-out vat as he has no money for a big house." It is also said that the God of Earth cannot afford a luxurious life; some rubbles of tiles or a broken vat set up on the ground can be the god's temple. However, the Lord of Earth is in charge of the land, which deserves people's worship on his birthday February 2nd, as a saying goes, "Even the God of Earth has his day".

5.Drawing Granaries on the Ground with Ash

This practice has a lot of names, such as "ash made granaries", "granary drawing", "granary filling" "making pleats", etc. As a time-honored custom on February 2nd, it appeared in South Song Dynasty, when poet Lu You wrote, "The sound of making ash granaries can be heard everywhere." In Yuan Dynasty, Zhao Mengfu wrote in his poem *To Her Grace: On Farming and Weaving*, "The ash is spread following the old practice, around the doors and along the lanes; by doing this I sincerely make a wish, may a year of harvest come to us." It is evident that the practice of drawing ash-made granaries was already popular in Song and Yuan Dynasties.

This practice has long been observed in North China, which is passed down by generations but seldom seen in nowadays. The plant ash used in this practice are often prepared on the first day of the year or before January 15th. They would be spread in the courtyard and posed into shapes of granary. On the morning of February 2nd, the head of the family carries the plant ash with dustpan and walks around the yard while gently striking the edges of the dustpan so as to spread the ash on the ground; the plant ash is well distributed into ash lines of one and half *cun* (1/3 decimetre) and form a circle, which represents the granary. In some places, people would use shovel to spread the ash. When the "granary" is finished, some wheat, millets

五、打囤

打囤，又称"打灰囤""围仓""围仓囤""画仓""填仓""打露囤""旋褙子"等，是一项历史久远的二月二节俗。早在南宋时期此俗就已出现，诗人陆游有"处处遥闻打囤声"的诗句。元代赵孟頫《题耕织图奉懿旨撰·二月》诗云："散灰沿旧俗，门径环周遭。所冀岁有成，殷勤在今朝。"可见，二月二"围仓"习俗在宋元时期已经广泛流行。

打囤之俗长期盛行于我国北方各省，现在仍有传承，但已不多见。打囤多用大年初一当天或正月十五前烧成的草木灰，在场院、家院内撒成若干仓形的图案。二月二清晨，当家的用簸箕盛上草木灰，用木棒轻轻敲打簸箕边沿，使其有规律地散落成约一寸半宽的灰线，边打边走，让灰线围成一圆圈，即为"囤"或"仓"。也有的地方用锨锄灰直接撒成仓囤形。打好囤，在中间放少许麦子、谷子、高粱等五谷杂粮，有的直接放在地上，也有先在中间挖一小坑，再放入粮食，上覆以石片砖瓦。撒好的灰囤就代表着家里的粮仓，寓意囤高粮满丰年在望。还有的地区，要在灰囤外沿画上梯子，叫"竖梯子"或"上粮"，以示囤高粮多。

有些地方将打灰囤与祀神仪式结合在一起进行，如黑龙江珠河就是在二月一日于庭院内祀仓神，并撒灰作仓廒形，里

and broomcorn are placed inside it or simply on the ground, sometimes a small pit was dug to place these grains with a tile covering on it. The ash-made granary represents the family grain barns; to fulfill it means that the family granary will be full in the coming year. In some places, outside the ash-made granary, an ash-made ladder is drawn to show that the "granary" is high with a great many grains stored.

In some places, this practice is combined with the worship of gods. For instance, in Zhuhe, Heilongjiang Province, on February 1st, people worship the God of Granary in their courtyard and spread the ash into the shape of granary with grains

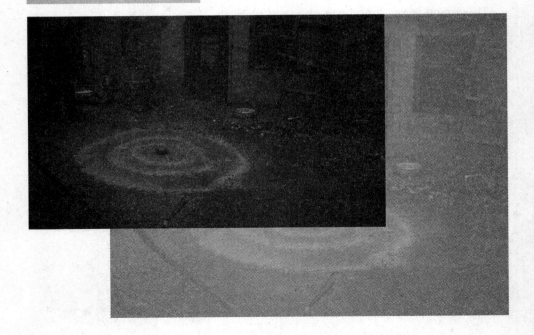

placed in it, which means a good harvest this year. In Dongming County in Heze, Shandong Province, after making the ash-granary, people burn incenses in front of it and offer sacrifice as well as fireworks to worship the Dragon God and pray for a harvest year. In Laiyang and Laixi, people celebrate the birthday of Lady Granary by putting a steamed bun or corn bun in each of the ash-made circles, and burning incense while chanting, "We offer the buns to your Grace, Lady Granary, please bless our barns to be full of grains."

Besides predicting and praying for the harvest in the future, the practice has some special connotations. For example, in Qufu, Shandong Province, the fact that someone fails to build a good social relationship and has very few friends is said to be the result of his failing to draw a nice ash-made granary. In Tai'an district, this practice is called "beating the dustpan", and the ash surrounding the house are indication of unity and friendship, which is described in local proverb "beating the dustpan on February 2nd brings good luck". The young wife married less than three years should not stay outside her husband's house on the very day in case she should be left outside the ash-made circle; on this occasion, the circle seems to suggest a protection of the family and marks the family borders. In Huaibei, Anhui Province, spreading ash is also related to women's wish to have more children. Before sunrise on February 2nd, when newly married women and

面还放杂粮少许,含有祈年报成的意思。在山东菏泽东明县,围好囤后,人们还要在粮囤前烧香、摆供和放爆竹以祭龙神,祈愿有个丰收年。莱阳、莱西等地称该日为满囤姑姑生日,每个灰囤中要放一个馒头或者窝窝头,上插一枝香,祭祀满囤姑姑,并唱念:"大囤满,小囤流,满囤姑姑滚馇馏(即窝窝头)。"

打囤围仓除了用以占卜丰歉、祈求丰收之外,还具有一些特别的内涵。如在山东曲阜地区,倘若有人社会交往不顺,没落下好人缘,会归之于二月二的仓囤没有围好。泰安地区,打囤叫"打簸箕",在房宅外的周遭撒一圈灰,喻示团结人,并形成一句歇后语"二月二打簸箕——囤(为)得好"。结婚不出三年的媳妇,这一天是不能住在婆家外面的,以免被围在仓外。此时,围仓似乎又喻示着家园边界的设置。在安徽淮北,撒灰还与妇女的祈育习俗联系在一起。

不论是新过门的媳妇，还是没有生育的媳妇，在二月二回娘家前，要在当天早晨日出前头不梳脸不洗，装一斗青灰来到打谷场，里三层外三层地撒上几道圆圈，俗信此举可以祈育。二月二打圈，不仅寄托了人们对于风调雨顺、五谷丰登、美满吉祥的强烈愿望，具有种种信仰色彩，人们还可以通过对打圈活动的亲手操作，感受到把握幸福、品味生活的一种艺术美感。

六、驱除虫害

惊蛰前后，春回大地，在农耕开始之际，也是百虫出蛰、蠢蠢欲动的时候。在二月二这天，民间有许多除虫的岁时活动。

1.撒灰

撒灰驱虫是二月二的一项重要仪式。灰多用灶灰。民国十九年（1930年）辽宁《盖平县志》载，当地二月二日"侵晨，家家用灶灰在庭院中多作大圆圈形，名'撒灰圈'。盖

nonparous women go to visit their parents, they would carry a basket of ash to the threshing ground and spread the ash into three circles, one in another, without combing their hair or washing their faces. It is believed that by doing so, they will have more children in the coming year. The practice of drawing "granary" circles on the ground represents people's strong wishes for favorable weather, a good harvest and a happy life; it serves as a belief in daily life; when people experience the whole process of drawing the ash-made granary, they will feel the aesthetic sense of art in their pursuit of happiness and taste of life.

6.Getting away from Pests

When spring finds its way back to the earth before and after the Day of Waking of Insects, and before the beginning of farm work, it is time for the insects and worms to come out of their hidden place. Therefore, on February 2nd, there were a variety of practice to get rid of some pests.

a.Spreading Ash

Spreading ash to drive away the insects is one of the important rituals on February 2nd. The ash is collected from kitchens. In 1930, *Chronicles of Gaiping County* in Liaoning Province wrote, "On February 2nd every household draws a huge circle in the backyard of their houses with kitchen ash, as it is called ash-made granary; since scutigers, scorpions, insects and ants all go out at this time of year, people have them surrounded by ash circles so as to keep them away from doing harm to mankind". The practice is prevailing in Hebei, Henan, Shanxi, Shandong, Shaanxi, Hubei, Gansu, Sichuan, Zhejiang and Guangdong. In Gaoyi, Hebei Province, people spread the ash at the root of walls to get rid of poisonous scorpions while chanting, "Spreading the ash along the root of walls on the second day of February keeps scorpions and centipedes away." In the evening, children burn the paper money and lampwick outside the door, which is said to be a see-off to scorpions and centipedes. In Mi County of Henan Province, people surround their houses with firewood ash to keep the Five Insects at bay. In Zhang County, Gansu Province, the spreading of ash in courtyard is called "forbidding the insects". In Ansai, Shaanxi Province, the similar practice is called "surrounding the dragons", or "surrounding the scutigers". In the middle and south of Shaanxi, the old would spread plant ash in every room, while beating on the dustpan and chanting, "On February 2nd, ashes in the dustpan drive insects and ants out of the house", which is thought to be a way to get rid of the insects. In Shandong Province, when people are drawing granary with ash, they would leave some ash along the root of walls in the courtyard, chanting, "On February 2nd, ash is spread; scorpions and centipedes die in piles", so as to keep away the insects as well as the bad luck. In Dongming district, such ritual and practice is much

以二月惊蛰，蛇蝎、虫蚁蠕蠕渐动，用灰圈包围镇压之，不欲其肆行妨害于人也”。这种做法在河北、河南、山西、山东、陕西、湖北、甘肃、四川、浙江、广东等地相当普遍。在河北高邑，将灰撒在墙根，以避蝎毒，而且还要边撒边念叨：“二月二，围墙根，蝎子蚰蜒不上身。”晚上，小孩子把纸钱和灯捻在门外烧掉，叫作“送蝎子蚰蜒”。在河南密县，人们用柴灰围屋，叫“避五瘟”。在甘肃漳县，也是在院子周围撒灰线，称为“禁蛰虫”。陕西安塞，同样的活动叫“围龙”，也叫“围蚰蜒”。在关中和陕南一带，老年人一边把草木灰撒在每间屋里，一边会敲着簸箕唱：“二月二，灰簸箕，虫虫蚂蚁飞出去！”以为这样可驱除虫蚁。在山东地区，撒灰围囤时不忘在院落墙根下撒一些，边撒边说“二月二，撒青灰，蝎子蚰蜒死成堆”，试图以此驱虫辟邪。在东明一带，撒灰驱虫仪式饶有趣味。初二日天黑前，孩子们纷纷去掏灰，把家里所有的墙根都撒上灰，叫作"围墙根儿"。男女孩童边撒边唱带有相互示威性质的游戏儿歌，小女孩唱道："围，围，围墙根，蝎子出来光蜇小小（方言，男孩），不蜇小妮（方言，女孩）！"小男孩则唱："围，围，围墙根，蝎子出来不蜇小小，光蜇小妮！"边围边吵，互不相让。

除了撒草木灰外，有些地方还时兴撒石灰。如在四川绵竹，就将石灰撒于住宅墙脚，以辟毒虫。在广东始兴，称二月二为"冻虫节"，在窟或一切器用之物周围撒石灰，以为可令虫蚁不侵。在浙江衢州市常山地区，二月二当天如果打雷下雨的话，就拍拍被褥赶虱子跳蚤，并且在墙边角落里撒下一些生石灰，赶走虫蚁。在山西翼城，有的人家会在二月二这天煮蔓菁汤，遍洒屋内壁间，叫作"禁百虫"；村民自发来到各家门口，向院内洒以米羹，门前撒以石灰，称作"禳瘟"。

2.击梁床门户

二月二日清早，用棍棒、扫帚或者鞋子敲打

more interesting. Before the nightfall on February 2nd, children would go collecting the ash and spread it along the root of the walls in their houses, which is called "ash spreading". Boys and girls then compete with and scare each other by singing ballads. Girls would sing, "Ash spreading, ash spreading, to the boys are coming the scorpions!" And boys in turn would sing, "Ash spreading, ash spreading, to the girls are coming the scorpions!" Neither side is willing to admit a failure; the game is going on and on as they do the ash spreading.

Besides plant ash, many places choose to spread lime. In Mianzhu, Sichuan Province, lime is spread around the houses to prevent poisonous insects. People in Shixing, Guangdong Province, name February 2nd as "Freezing Insects Day", and spread lime on all of the implements to prevent insects and ants. In Changshan area of Quzhou, Zhejiang Province, if it is raining and thundering on February 2nd, people would pat their quilt to get rid of fleas, and spread lime in corners of the house to prevent ants. In Yicheng, Shanxi Province, some families would cook turnip soup and sprinkle it onto the walls inside the house to prevent all sorts of insects; villagers also sprinkle rice soup into their own backyard and spread lime in front of the door, which is called "staying away from illness".

b.Beating the Roof Beams, Beds and Doorframe

On the morning of February 2nd, people use sticks, brooms and shoes to beat the beams, walls, doorframes and beds to expel the insects as a common festival practice. In many regions, people believe that beating the beams on this day will frighten away the mice, which is called "beams beating, mice expelling". In Chaoyang, Liaoning Province, people beat the beams and doorframes to keep the scorpions and scutigers away. In Gu'an, Hebei Province, before the daybreak, children are asked to beat the edges of the beds and pillows with a stick to frighten away the snakes and scorpions.

While beating, people also chant some ballads. In Qingyun, Shandong Province, the chanting is, "beat the bed edges on February 2nd, scorpions and scutigers all disappear; beat the pillows on that day, scorpions and snakes all run away." In Heze, people beat the beams, bed edges and old gourd ladles while chanting, "Beat the beams on the second day of February, scorpions and scutigers hide nowhere; beat the gourd ladles on that day, scorpions and scutigers all get blind."

Besides expelling the insects, beating the beams and beds has other functions as well. For instance, in the middle of Liaoning Province, people get up early to beat the beams with a long rod, which is called "beating dragon's head", as a gesture of waking up the sleeping dragon. In Bozhou, Anhui Province, an auspicious rhyme goes with the practice, "Beat

梁头、墙壁、门户、床炕等处，是一种十分普遍的活动，其目的亦为驱除害虫。在许多地区，人们认为在这天敲打房梁，能惊吓老鼠，谓之"击梁辟鼠"。在辽宁朝阳，人们会用棒棍敲打过梁、门户等，以避蛇蝎与蚰蜒。在河北固安，每家在天未明时分，就让小孩用木棍敲炕沿或枕头，以惊走蛇蝎等毒虫。

人们在击打时，常常伴以歌谣念唱。如在山东庆云，二月二日击炕，要边打边说："二月二日打炕沿，蝎子蚰蜒不见面。二月二日打炕头，蝎子蚰蜒全不留。"在菏泽，人们击打房梁、床沿和破瓢，边打边唱："二月二，敲房梁，蝎子蚰蜒无处藏。二月二，敲瓢碴，蝎子蚰蜒双眼瞎。"

除驱虫外，击梁敲床等还有另外一些功能。如在辽中一带，晨起以竿敲梁，谓之"敲龙头"，喻示要敲醒仍在沉睡的龙。在安徽亳州，敲梁时往往伴随着"二月二，敲梁头，金子银子往家流"的吉祥语。在山东郓城和临朐等地，人们会用灰在屋内撒成一个正方形的钱柜，内放一枚制钱或银元，然后老太太用木棒敲打门砧和门框，边敲边唱："二月二，敲门砧，金子银子往家滚。二月二，敲门框，金子银子往家扛。"济宁一带亦有此"敲财"习俗。二月二这天各家吃过晚饭，大人怂恿自家孩子拿出事先准备好的小木棍，一边敲打着门枕、门框等，一边吟唱："二月二，敲门砧，金子银子往家滚。二月二，敲门框，金子银子往家扛。"此后还会敲打其他物件，甚至竞相跑到胡同里或大街上比赛，看谁敲的、唱的花样多。此时的"敲财"，已不仅仅意在祈富，而是具有了更多的游戏色彩。

3.照虫烛

照虫烛，即燃香或者点火以驱虫。在黑龙江双城，人们在门窗、炕沿各处插香，认为这样能熏死虫类。在辽宁安东，则用

the beams on February 2nd, gold and silver flows into the house." In Yuncheng and Linqu, Shandong Province, people spread the ash in the house to form a square shape representing the money locker and place a piece of copper or silver coin within, then elder women of the family would beat the doorsill and doorframe while chanting, "Beat the doorsill on February 2nd, gold and silver rush into the door; beat the doorframe on this day, gold and silver is carried into the house." In Ji'ning, there is a custom of "beating for wealth". On February 2nd, after dinner, children are encouraged to beat the thresholds and doorframe with small wood sticks prepared in advance while chanting a similar ballad as the previous one mentioned above. Later, they would find other things to beat, and even run into the lanes and streets to compete with each other; the child that beats the most things and sings the best wins. "Beating for wealth" in this sense is not only a practice to pray for more wealth, but also a game to entertain the public.

c.Lighting up the Candles

Lighting up the candles is also called burning incense or lighting the fire to expel insects. In Shuangcheng, Heilongjiang Province, people will place the incenses near the doors, the windows and along the bedsides to kill the insects by the odor In

Andong, Liaoning Province, the remained incenses are used to smoke the beds to get rid of insects. In Kaiyuan, all households burn the short joss sticks and put them into cracks and rifts of the house to drive away the insects.[1] In Liaoyang, Haicheng and Xifeng of Liaoning Province, candles are lighted up in the dark corners of the house on the night of February 2nd, to get rid of the insects, which is how the practice get its name as "lighting up the candles". In Lishu, Jilin Province, it is in the morning of February 2nd, when all households light up incenses in every corner of the house to prevent insects and ants; when night falls, candles are also lit in the dark corners. In Lianyungang, Jiangsu Province, on the night of February 2nd, children would light up torches in the fields and throw them up into the sky while chanting loudly, "Torch, torch, my colored glaze, send the locust to the hell."

d.Smoking the Insects

In some places, people have the tradition of smoking the insects with cakes fried by sesame oil, which is believed to keep implements from being damaged by moths. According to *The Official Notes of Yongping (Qinhuangdao)*, the sesame oil cake is used to smoke the moths away from eating the furniture, and to prevent insects and ants. The

残香熏床炕各处，曰"熏虫"。在开原一带，"各家皆用短香燃火，遍置于屋内有罅隙处，谓能避毒虫"[1]。照虫烛多在初二夜晚进行，如辽宁辽阳、海城、西丰等地，都是在房屋中的黑暗角落点燃蜡烛，名为"照虫烛"，以此驱除虫子。在吉林梨树，则是初二日早晨，各家各户在室内四角处点燃香火，以驱虫蚁；到了夜晚，就在黑暗处点燃蜡烛，名曰"照虫蜡"。在江苏连云港一带，二月二日晚上，孩子们要到农田里点燃火把，一个接一个地往空中抛，口里大声喊着："火把火把琉璃灯，大小蝗虫都死清。"

4.熏虫

有些地方，人们在二月二有用香油煎糕来熏虫的传统，认为以此法可使物品不为虫所蛀。《永平府志》中说："用香油煎糕熏虫，则物不蛀，且以避虫蚁。"山东有用煎糕

[1]Edited by Ding Shiliang, Zhao Fang. *Local Chronicles in China: Information Compilation on Folk Customs*, Volume of Mid-South China. Beijing Library Publishing House, 1991, p.165.

[1]丁世良，赵放主编：《中国地方志民俗资料汇编·中南卷》，北京：北京图书馆出版社，1991年，第165页。

熏虫的习俗，用正月留下的年糕煎成饼状吃，也可煎一般面饼，叫"煎糕熏虫"。在邹城一带，二月二这天要煎鱼驱虫。早在光绪十八年《邹县志》卷二引乾嘉时王仲磊《邹鲁岁时记》中有记载："二月二日……炒大豆食之，烹鱼，曰熏虫。"时至今日，当地煎鱼的习俗还普遍存在着。每年二月初二清晨，在太阳出来之前要把鱼煎好，人们解释说："二月二要煎鱼，以前没有农药，就用它来熏虫。"可见，煎鱼的目的是为了防止庄稼生虫害。

5.贴画符图

在许多地区的二月二节俗中，剪纸、贴符、画葫芦等民间艺术形式也常被用来驱除虫蚁。如在辽宁兴城，妇女们会在二月二前后剪红纸贴于墙壁，即引龙驱虫之意。又据民国二十三年（1934年）《奉天通志》，妇女会用绵制成鸡形，悬挂室中，以为能够避蚰蜒、制虫蚁。在山西东南地区，人们习惯贴画葫芦于屋壁，

practice is also preserved in Shandong, where rice cakes left in January are made into pancakes and fried for food, which is also used to keep the insects away. In Zoucheng, on the second day of February, people have fish fried to keep away the insects. The second chapter of *Chronicles of Zou County* in 1892 cited from *The Notes of Seasons of States Zou and Lu* by Wang Zhonglei of Qianlong and Jiajing reign, "On February 2nd, people eat fried beans and fried fish to keep the insects away." Till this day, it is still a prevailing custom to fry fish on the day; it is explained that there was no pesticide for the farmers to kill the insects before, so the fried fish of February 2nd is used to smoke them away. Therefore, frying fish becomes a common way to prevent crops being destroyed by insects.

e.Posting Pictures and Amulets

In many places, forms of folk art such as paper-cutting, amulets posting and gourd drawing are all used to celebrate February 2nd and get rid of insects and ants. In Xingcheng, Liaoning Province, women post the cut-red-papers on the walls to invite dragons and keep away insects. According to *Chronicles of Fengtian* in 1934, women weave silk floss into cloth in the shape of rooster, and hang it in the room to get rid of scutigeras and insects. In the southeast of Shanxi, people used to draw a gourd with the five poisonous insects (snakes, scorpions, centipedes, millipedes and spiders) on the walls to keep away all kinds of insects. In Xiangning, Shanxi

Province, people post amulets to prevent scorpions. In Suzhou, Jiangsu Province, the same practice is followed as amulets are posted on tables, chairs, and chests while small children chanting "post the amulet of scutiger, bad insects are doomed to die".

f.Feeding the Insects

In Nantong, Jiangsu Province, sticky rice, corns, sorghums, buckwheat and sesames are ground into flour and made into various shapes, such as birthday peaches, apples, chickens, ducks, pigs, dogs, cattle and sheep; after the flour-made "animals" are steamed, they are stringed together by bamboo rods and placed in the fields, as it is believed that if the God of Insects eat these offerings, it will not hurt the crops anymore. In Xingning, Lanshan, Jiahe and Leiyang of Hunan Province, it is a common practice to "seal the birds' beaks". On February 1st, sticky rice and sorghums are made into special gnocchi which are served on breakfast; the rest are stringed by bamboo branches and placed in the fields to feed the birds. It is hoped that the sticky gnocchi can seal the birds' beaks so that they won't be able to eat up the crops. It is evident that the purpose of this practice is to protect the crops from insects.

以避百虫，葫芦中装有蛇、蝎、蜈蚣、蚰蜒、蜘蛛等五种毒虫。在山西乡宁，人们会贴符以厌蝎。在江苏苏州，人们在桌、床、椅、箱等家具上贴"蜓蚰榜"，贴时小孩在旁边唱"贴上蜓蚰榜，害虫都死光"之谣。

6.喂百虫

在江苏南通，家家户户把糯米、玉米、高粱、荞麦、芝麻粉做成寿桃、苹果、鸡、鸭、猪、狗、牛、羊等形状，蒸熟后插在青竹梢上，于黄昏时分送到田头，认为百虫之神吃了斋果就不来伤害庄稼了。在湖南兴宁、蓝山、嘉禾、耒阳一带，都时兴"粘雀口"或"糊鸟嘴"之俗。二月初一日，用糯米和高粱做成糍团，在早晨食用一部分后，将剩余的用竹枝穿上，插到田间，意思是糊住鸟嘴，不让鸟雀吃庄稼苗。其保护庄稼不受害虫侵害的目的十分明显。

七、试犁、舞春牛、饭牛

山东地区曾广泛流行二月二春耕试犁仪式。在黄县一带，自二月二起开始农作，择日进行试犁。海阳等地二月二试犁前，扶犁人先礼拜犁具，并唱喜歌："犁破新春土，牛踩丰收亩；春种一粒粟，秋收万颗子。"然后牵着牛到田间象征性地耕一耕，充满辛苦也充满希望的一年劳作就这样开始了。

每年二月二开耕时节，粤西山区农村便盛行"舞春牛"。"春牛"一般由两个演员伴舞，一人舞牛头，一人舞牛身和牛尾。"牛头"用木头或竹篾扎制，外形比真牛头大一倍，"牛身"用布制成，遮住里边的演员。"舞春牛"是一种历史悠久、乡土气息浓郁的民间舞蹈，同时也有表演唱作，其角色有农夫（耕夫）、牛郎（看牛仔）、太公、村姑、白鹤、春牛，乐队由4人组成。打

7. Ploughing, Cattle Dancing and Cattle Feeding

The ritual of spring ploughing on February 2nd was once prevailing in Shandong Province. In Huang County, farmers began their work in the fields on February 2nd, and they would choose the luckiest day to start the ploughing practice. In Haiyang, before the ploughing on that day, the farmer would first salute to the plough, and chant, "The plough breaks the spring soil while the cattle walk on the fields; I sow a seed in the soil now and in autumn, I will have a good harvest." Then the farmer will walk the cattle in the fields and make a gesture of ploughing, which marks the beginning of a year's farm work with pains and gains.

On the second day of February, when the farming season begins, people would celebrate by doing the "spring cattle dance" in the countryside of the mountainous areas in the west of Guangdong Province. The "cattle" is played by two actors, one in charge of the head and the other the body and tail. The head is made of wood or bamboos, which is twice as large as the head of a real cattle; the body is made by cloth, which covers the actor inside. "Spring cattle dance" is a folk dance that boasts a long history and a close relationship with people's daily life; it is more of a role-play performance than a simple dance: the roles include a farmer, a cowboy, a grandfather, a village girl, a white crane and the cattle, with a band made up of four people. When the percussion music is on, the cowboy pulls the "cattle" onto the stage, followed by the farmer with his plough, the girl with a basket full of flowers, the grandfather with a cane in his hand and the white crane by the side of the cattle; they march on while singing and dancing, which is one of the most hilarious occasions.

In Lianyungang, Jiangsu Province, on February 2nd, the cattle are allowed to take a rest and have a good meal, as it is believed that "the cattle must be fed well on February 2nd as they have gone through hard work and severe scolds for a whole year". In Suqian, Jiangsu Province, people treat livestock such as cattle, horses and donkeys in a nice way: pancakes offered to the God of Earth on the twentieth day of the twelfth month of the lunar year are left to feed these livestock, as it is said that only in this way can people maintain the prosperity of the farm.

8.Dropping the Vegetable Seeds

In Zhejiang district, the custom of dropping the vegetable seeds is very popular as a folk saying goes like this, "On February 2nd when the dragon raises its head, His Majesty ploughs the soil while his servants drive the cattle; Her Grace brings the meal and dessert, and the minister drops the seeds; ploughing and weeding in spring and summer brings the harvest and happy days in autumn."

击乐一响，牛郎牵春牛出场，农夫驾着犁随后，村姑担花篮，太公执手杖，白鹤随牛左右，载歌载舞，十分热闹喜庆。

在江苏连云港，二月二这天是不让牛干活的，要做一顿好饭喂牛，所谓"打一千，骂一万；二月二，吃顿饭"。在江苏宿迁，人们对牛、马、驴等大牲畜十分优待，并把腊月二十祭灶供的大饼留到二月二给它们吃，据说这样才能槽头兴旺。

八、下菜种

在浙江地区，比较时兴在二月二这天下瓜茄菜种的习俗。民间有这样的说法："二月二，龙抬头，天子耕地臣赶牛；正宫娘娘来送饭，当朝大臣把种丢。春耕夏耘率天下，五谷丰登太平秋。"

2 / 节期饮食
Festival Foods

"过了十五过十六，过了十六就照旧。"这是老百姓对年节大好时光似水流逝的无奈。一般人家从大年初一这天起，就享受着一种坐吃成穿的日子，这情形一直延续到正月十六。特别是在饮食上，一般过了十六就改换成平日的吃食，这叫"换饭"。但是到了"换饭"之时，并不是把过年吃的东西全都吃完，主妇必会留出一点面食，至少留出一碗年糕，到二月二再端上饭桌，使全家人再享受一次过年的滋味。别小看这碗年糕，它代表了过大

"When the fifteenth day of January passes, the sixteenth day comes; when the sixteenth day passes, everything goes back to its usual way again." The proverb expresses people's reluctance to say goodbye to the good time they spend in Spring Festival holiday. Normally, the whole family enjoy the idling time since the first day of the lunar year as they do not need to prepare food or worry about their clothes until the sixteenth day when the Spring Festival holiday is over. During the sixteen days of Spring Festival holiday, people have enough festival foods left; but after the sixteenth day, they have to go back to the normal diet, which is called "change the meals". But not all the festival foods are taken off the table by then, the housewife will put away some noodles or a bowl of New Year rice cake at least, and bring them back to the table on February 2nd to relive the New Year mood. The bowl of rice cake may be too little for the stomach, but it does bring back the tender memories of the Spring Festival which console people's hearts and add more fun to their life.

Besides rice cakes, there are a variety of festival foods for February 2nd, all fitting into the festival nature of this special day with their unique flavors. As February 2nd is considered as the day when the dragon raises its head, a lot of festival foods are related to dragons, for instance, boiled dumplings are called "dragon's ears", pigs' heads are called "dragons' heads" and spring cakes are called "dragons' scales". February 2nd is also a day when insects are coming out. People do all they can to get away from those insects and animals that do harm to people's health and daily life. As a result, the names of food are often related with insects expelling, for example, fried seasoned beans are called "fried crabs' pincers", and steamed buns made from millets are called "biting crabs' heads". These names sound like witchcraft and indicate people's best wishes to get rid of the pests and pursue a healthy life.

1.Rice Cakes

Eating rice cakes is a popular practice on February 2nd; it is more than a sweet memory of

年的一抹温情，让人们的心灵得到些许慰藉，为普通的生活添几分韵味。

除了那碗年糕，二月二还有许多其他的饮食习俗。这些饮食根据二月二的节日性质而设置，因此具有独特的魅力。二月二日是"龙抬头"之时，许多食品便与龙牵扯在一起，比如吃水饺叫"吃龙耳"，吃猪头叫"吃龙头"，吃春饼叫"食龙鳞"等。二月二日是百虫蠢动之时，对于那些有害于人类健康和生活的昆虫动物，人们唯恐避之不及，总是想方设法加以驱除。饮食也往往被赋予驱虫的含义，成为驱虫的手段。比如炒料豆又叫"炒蟹子爪"、吃黄米馒头就是"咬蟹子头"等。这些带有巫术意味的食品名称，表达了人们驱除虫害、追求健康的美好愿望。

一、吃年糕

二月二吃年糕之俗流行甚广，它既是对过年的一种回味，又被人们赋予了多种功能。上海、江苏、浙江等许多地方，在二月初二这天有吃"撑腰糕"的习惯。"撑腰糕"其实就是年糕，俗信吃了年糕不腰痛，因此叫作"撑腰糕"。

the Spring Festival as people give various functions to it. In Shanghai, Jiangsu and Zhejiang, people eat "waist-support cakes" on February 2nd, which is a kind of rice cake. It is believed that rice cakes can prevent people from waist ache, which is how it gets a name as "waist support" cake. According to *Knowledge On Ancient Crops*, "On February 2nd, the birthday of the God of Earth, people eat fried rice cakes, which are called 'waist-supporting'."

旧时农村，春节一过，乡下的农活便忙开了，面朝黄土背朝天，弯腰鞠躬年复年。为了祈求在新的一年中能够不腰酸不背痛，要在二月二吃"撑腰糕"。这天一大早，农家妇女就淘好糯米放到外面吹到八分干，然后去磨粉，磨好粉回来开始做"撑腰糕"。糕做好了，煮起来也很讲究，要把它排在一只圆圆的小蒸笼里，

In countryside of the old days, when Spring Festival is over, the busy farming season is coming; farmers stoop over their fields, ploughing and tilling day after day. Therefore, they eat the "waist-supporting cakes" on February 2nd in hope of being free from waist soreness and backache. On the early morning of this day, housewives put the washed sticky rice outside the house for air drying, and then grind the rice into powders, which are made into the cakes. The process of cooking the cakes is a bit complicated, as the cakes are put in lines in a small round steamer, which is placed into the boiler and heated by soft fire. The cake takes the shape of human waist, which is oblate and sunken in the middle. In Xiangshan, Ningbo City, people eat fried rice cakes with grass seeds on February 2nd. The grass seeds refer to the seeds of milk vetch, which is believed to be helpful for women to get pregnant, as a saying goes, "Fried rice cake with milk vetch's seeds makes the wife have more babies." Eating rice cakes also implies a rise in career life as "rice" sounds like "rise". In Xiangshan, it is said that, "February 2nd is the time to eat rice cakes; the cake made of rice brings you a year-by-year rise." In Yuhang district, Hangzhou, on this day, rice cakes are made into the shape of silkworm in white or green (adding leaves of pumpkin or other green plants for the green color); when cooked, they are put into a tray and placed on the stovetop and a bowl of rice is put on a stool near the door, in this way people pray for a healthy growth of the silkworms.

2.Fried Seasoned Beans

It is very popular to fry kernels and beans on February 2nd. In Shandong Province, the practice of frying seasoned beans on February 2nd prevails. The seasoned beans are also called "scorpion beans", which are mainly the soybeans in salty or sweet flavor. Salty beans have been soaked in the

放在锅上用文火烧熟。从外形上看，"撑腰糕"状如人腰，呈扁圆形，中间稍凹，十分形象。在宁波象山地区，二月二这天通常要吃草籽炒年糕。草籽即紫云英。人们认为草籽炒年糕有利于妇女生育，有"草籽炒年糕，娘娘大卵泡"之谚。吃年糕，还意味着新年步步高升。象山俗谓"二月二，吃年糕，吃了年糕，年年高"。在杭州余杭地区，二月二这天人们会把糯米做成蚕宝宝的形状，蒸着吃。蒸糕的颜色有白色和绿色（当中加南瓜叶或者其他绿色植物），并且要摆一盆放在灶台上，盛一碗白米饭放在门口的板凳上，祭祀一番，祈求这一年蚕宝宝能够健康成长。

二、炒料豆

二月二炒麦、豆之俗流传甚广。在山东盛行二月二这天炒料豆，"炒料豆"又称"炒蝎豆"，其成分主要是黄豆，有咸、甜两种口味。咸的料豆是将黄豆在盐水中浸泡后炒制而成；甜的料豆则将黄豆在炒的过程中放上糖，将豆子炒成块，香脆可口。旧时，家家户户都要在二月二清晨太阳升起之前将料豆炒好，然后在屋内墙角撒上炒好的豆子（蝎子爪），意为蝎子不蜇人。在潍县、莱州等地将炒豆称作"报捷"，谐音"爆蜇"，是说吃了炒蝎豆，能保证一年不被蝎子蜇。郓城、鄄城等地称作"炒蝎子爪"，有俗语说"吃了蝎子爪，蝎子不用打"。泰安干脆直接叫"吃虫"，因为豆粒似虫卵，炒而食之，虫死人安。各地叫法不同，其实大同小异，都是为了规避蝎子、蚰蜒等害虫的侵害。在梁山地区，除了炒黄豆，还要炒面豆、炒玉米等，这些节令食品深受孩童喜爱，他们往往在清晨上学的路上，唱着歌谣挨家上门讨要："二月二炒蝎子爪，大娘婶子给一把。"在临沂费县，料豆除了用黄豆以外，还包括花生、高粱、玉米、小麦

salty water and then fried; sweet beans are fried with sugar and into crisp and tasty pieces. In the past, all families would get the beans prepared before sunrise and spread the fried beans, the so-called "scorpion's pincers", on the corners inside the house implying that the scorpions would not hurt people. In Wei County and Laizhou, the fried beans are called "baojie"(messengers of good news), a homophonic word of "baozhe"(stop the biting), which means staying away from the bites and stings of scorpions for the whole year if you eat the fried beans. In Yuncheng and Juancheng, the fried beans is called "fried scorpion's pincers" as in the proverb, "If you eat the scorpion's pincers, you are free from the scorpions." In Tai'an, eating fried beans are called "eating the insects", as the beans look like insect eggs; if the "eggs" are cooked and eaten, people can enjoy an insect-free spring. Though the names given to fried beans is different, the message delivered by these names is the same one, which is to protect people from harms done by scorpions and scutigers. In Liangshan district, besides fried soybeans, there are fried noodles and fired corns. Children love these festival foods, and they ask for them from door to door on their way to school while chanting, "Fried crab pincers on February 2nd, dear auntie please gives us a handful." In Fei County, Linyi district, seasoned beans include soybeans, peanuts, sorghum, corns and wheat; the five grains represent the "five dangerous insects" such as scorpions and scutigers etc. The way to fry these beans is as follows: first of all, soak the seasoned beans in the water to soften them; then string the beans with needle and threads; fry the strings of beans after the sunset, which is called by local people as "frying the five poisonous insects", implying toasting the pests to death. While frying and stirring, people would curse the poisonous insects and pray for healthy life. The fried seasoned beans are shared among neighbors, and it is believed that anyone eats the seasoned beans from seven households will live a hundred years.

3. "Dragon Beard Noodles" and Steamed "Dragon's Eggs"

Besides the fried seasoned beans, most of the festival foods on February 2nd are related with dragons, such as "dragon beard noodles", "dragon scales pancake", "dragon's ears", "dragon's teeth" "dragon's eggs" and "dragon's seeds", all of which are endowed with auspicious message.

In North China, noodles and dumplings are popular foods on February 2nd. In Beijing, eating dumplings is called "eating dragon's teeth", and eating the steamed meat with flour wrappers is called "eating the lazy dragons". In Ji'an, Jilin Province, dumplings are called "dragon's ears" and noodles are called "dragon beard". In Gucheng County, Hebei Province, generally people eat

等五种粮食，暗喻蝎子、蚰蜒等"五毒"。其做法是，先用水将料豆泡软，然后再用针线串成毒虫的样子，等到太阳落山后放到锅里翻炒，当地人称为"炒五毒"，意思是将毒虫炒死。在炒的过程中，还要说些诅咒毒虫、祈祷平安的话。炒完的料豆要分给街坊邻里相互品尝，有俗语道："谁吃了七家的料豆，便能长命百岁。"

三、食龙须面、蒸龙蛋

除了炒料豆以外，二月二的节日食俗大都与龙有关，如"龙须面""龙鳞饼""龙耳""龙牙""龙蛋""龙子"等，都有寓意吉祥的意思。

北方地区流行二月二吃面条、水饺。在北京地区，这一天吃水饺称"吃龙牙"，吃蒸肉卷子叫"吃懒龙"。在吉林辑安，吃水饺叫"吃龙耳"，吃面条叫"吃龙须"。在河北故城县，一般在二月二中午吃饺子或者饸子，据说在这一天，家里有儿子的吃饺子，儿子结婚后生的孩子"虎势"①；家里没儿子的，一般吃饸子，意思是和和美美，能招佳婿。河北南宫将吃水饺叫"吃龙角"，河北高邑将吃面条叫"挑龙头"。内蒙古呼和浩特市将吃水饺叫"按龙眼"。

在山东地区，滕县这天要蒸馍馍，名为"蒸龙蛋"。沂源一带习惯蒸大馒头，有的一锅仅蒸一个，俗称"花饽饽"，顶上有面制叶片和一枚大红枣，也有用手工或模具做成龙、虎、燕、兔和鱼等动物模样的面食。威海等地早起蒸糕，以祝春龙起蛰。河北张北，将吃猪头叫"吃龙头"，吃葱饼叫"食龙皮"，吃面条叫"食龙须"。晋南这天则必定要吃麻花、馓子，谓之"啃龙骨"。山西

①虎势：当地方言，结实有生气的意思。

dumplings or a cooked wheaten pastry called *Hezi* on the noon of February 2nd. It is said that boys of the family should eat dumplings, which implies that when they get married, they will have children as strong and lively as tigers (hushi)[1]; girls of the family, on the other hand, should eat the *Hezi*, which implies a harmonious life and a happy marriage in the future. In Nangong, Hebei Province, dumplings is called "dragon's horns"; in Gaoyi, Hebei Province, eating noodles is called "lifting dragon's head"; in Hohhot, the Inner Mongolia Autonomous Region, eating dumplings is called "pressing down the dragon's eyes".

In Shandong Province, people in Teng County steam the MoMo (a flour-made food like buns) and call it "steamed dragon's eggs". It is a custom to make steamed buns in Yiyuan region, one bun in one pot, which is called "flower-like buns" with a flour-made "leaf" and a big red date on it; flour-made dragons, tigers, swallows, rabbits and fish are created by hands or moulds. In places like Weihai, people get up early to make steamed cakes as a way to celebrate the waking up of the spring dragon. In Zhangbei, Hebei Province, eating pig's head is called "eating dragon's head", and pancakes with green onions are called "eating dragon's skins" and noodles is called "eating dragon's beard". In south of Shanxi, on February 2nd people must eat fried dough twists, which is called "biting the

[1]Hushi, local dialect, referring to a state of strength and liveliness.

dragon's bones". People in Lüliang region love to eat pancakes on that day, which is called "tearing off dragon's skin". It is hoped that the food named after dragon will bring luck and fortune to those who eat it. In some places, on the contrary, people show their respect to dragons by prohibiting food that relates to dragons. For example, in places like Qufu, people prefer steamed stuffed buns to noodles and millet porridge, as noodles are called "dragon's beard" and millets "dragon's seeds"; some even believe that eating noodles is "breaking dragon's tendon ", which is a big disgrace to dragons.

吕梁地区喜食煎饼，称为"揭龙皮"。人们希望在吃下这些以龙命名的食物之后，可以沾沾"龙"的神气，是一种寓意吉祥的表达。但也有些地方，禁食这些被附会上"龙"的寓意的食物，是敬龙畏龙的表现。如曲阜等地讲究吃大包子，不吃面，不喝小米饭，因为面条是"龙须"，小米是"龙子"，吃了怕影响龙，也有的地方认为吃面条会"抽龙筋"。

四、春饼

北方地区，二月二多食春饼。当地吃春饼时要配"合菜"。所谓"合菜"，是将瘦肉丝与各样蔬菜如菠菜、豆芽菜、蒜黄等合在一起炒熟而成。食用时将春饼一分为二，抹上甜面酱，配上大葱，再夹上"合菜"，卷成筒状，手托而食。在山东郓城等地，人们认为烙饼可以铺囤底，盖囤尖，防鼠防蛀，确保粮仓完好。河北高阳一带有吃"摊煎饼"的习俗，"摊煎饼"也叫"菜饼子""摊片儿"、咸食等。邯郸一

4.Spring Pancakes

In North China, people also eat spring pancakes on February 2nd. According to local practice, the spring pancakes are often eaten with "mixed stew", which is a special dish mixing shredded meat with various vegetables, such as spinach, bean sprouts and garlic. When eaten, a spring pancake is divided into two layers and a sweet sauce made of fermented flour is spread on both layers; shallots and the mixed stew are put between the two layers; the pancakes are then rolled into tubular shape and sent into mouth with one hand holding from behind. In Yuncheng, Shandong Province, people believe that baked pancakes can be used to pave the floor of the granary and cover the top of it to prevent mice and moths and ensure that the granary is in a good condition. In Gaoyang, Hebei Province, the practice of "Tan (making) pancakes" is observed, which is

also called "Cai (making) pancakes" "Tan slices" or "salty food". In Handan district, a saying goes like this, "A strong wind blows on February 2nd; firewood is collected and pancakes are made." In most parts of Henan, people make pancakes with iron pan or griddle; the iron pot has to be upturned to get the pancake out, as it is believed that the flour paste inside the pan represents the earth, the upturned pan looks like the heaven in the time of chaos, and when the paste sticks to the pan, the earth is patching and healing the heaven, just like what the legend has said about the beginning of the world and human being. [1]

5.Eating Pig's Head

In some places of Heilongjiang, Jilin, Liaoning and Hebei Province, people used to kill pigs at the end of the old year and left pigs' heads and feet till February 2nd of the new year to eat, as described in a proverb, "On February 2nd, when dragon raises its head, rains come from the sky and stream on the ground; it's time to eat the pig's head." It is believed that eating meats from pigs' heads, washing head and having a haircut on February 2nd all indicate a good start in a new year. Besides, meat from pigs' heads is also taken as "dragon's meat", which is said to keep the family safe and sound. One or two days before February 2nd, housewives of the

①Zhao Jianmin. *Pancakes Patch the Sky. Folklore Studies*, 1999(2):p.85.

带流传着"二月二，刮大风，拾干柴，摊煎饼"的民谣。在河南的大部分地区，人们用铁锅或鏊子摊煎饼吃。摊煎饼时，要把铁锅倒扣过来，把煎饼倒出。人们认为，面糊可代表泥土，锅倒扣过来，像混沌中的天，而煎饼贴在锅上，有补天之意。[1]

五、吃猪头

在黑龙江、吉林、辽宁、河北等省的一些地方，各家习惯将年末宰杀的肥猪头、猪蹄留到二月二日再吃，有"二月二，龙抬头，天上下雨地下流，家家户户吃猪头"的谚语。人们认为，二月二吃猪头肉、洗头、剃头，预示新年有个好的开始，而且食"猪头肉"即表示食龙肉，可保家人平安健康。在二月初二的前一两

①赵建民：《煎饼补苍天》，《民俗研究》1999年第2期，第85页。

天，家中主妇就要提前把猪头收拾妥当，烀熟以备食用。有经验的主妇在猪头即将烀熟之时，时常要用筷子插猪头，倘若能插透即表示肉已经熟透。可见，这个看似简单的活儿不是谁都能做好的，必须由家中有经验的主妇来完成。

family would have the pig head cleaned and cooked. Experienced housewives would put chopsticks into the pig's head when it is boiled, if the chopsticks can penetrate the head, the meat is ready to eat. The job is not so easy as it seems, therefore, it is often done by the experienced housewife in the family.

吃猪头肉的时候，通常是用手将熟肉撕下或是用刀将熟肉切片，将大蒜拍成小碎瓣，倒入酱油，以肉蘸酱油食用。烀熟的猪头肉，每个部位吃起来都颇有讲究。例如猪的上牙槽，当地人称"猪鹊（当地人读音同'巧'）儿"，通常是要留给家里的年轻人吃，所谓"吃猪鹊儿，手巧儿"。当地人

When eating meat of pig's head, the usual way is to tear off the meat by hands or cut the meat into slices with a knife; the garlic is squashed into petals and put into a saucer of soy sauce, where the meat is dipped before sent into the month. Every part of the boiled pig's head has its special meaning: the upper alveolar ridge is called "pig magpie (qiao)" (a homophonic word in local dialect of "clever"), which is often left to the young people in the family to eat, as it is believed that those who eat pig magpie are deft and clever in their work. Meat on pig's face is left to people who have trouble with their eyes, as it is said that if the eyes have red dots in them, the meat will wipe them out and the eyes will be cured in this way.

通常认为，年轻人吃了猪鹤儿，做起活儿来会做什么像什么。"猪拱嘴儿"（即猪脸肉）通常要留给眼睛有疾的人，当地人通常认为，倘若眼睛上长了红点，吃过猪拱嘴儿后，就会把红点"拱"掉，眼疾就会好转。

6.Leaf Mustard Rice

In the suburb of cities and towns of Zhejiang, the festival food on February 2nd is leaf mustard rice. Leaf mustards are chopped with knife and cooked with rice, which is said to be able to improve the the eyesight and prevent from getting from getting furuncle.

The origin of leaf mustard rice comes from an interesting story. It is said that one day, Emperor Qianlong dressed like populace to travel around and collected some unfiltered public opinions. When he visited a farmer's house in Huizhou, a young man whose last name is Zhang greeted him and invited him to dinner. Zhang is a learned student, but couldn't afford a trip to the capital to take the imperial examination due to his poverty. When preparing the dinner, Zhang found the rice left in vat is not enough for a meal and there were no dishes either. An idea struck him as he asked his wife to get the stove ready and he left the house into the garden; he returned with some fresh leaf mustards, which he

六、芥菜饭

在浙江城乡郊区，二月二最普遍的饭是芥菜饭。将芥菜用刀切碎，与米一起煮饭，叫作"芥菜饭"，据说吃了以后可以明目，不生疮疖。

关于芥菜饭的来历，当地还有一个有趣的传说：一天，乾隆皇帝微服察访民情，到徽州一农户家中，发现一名饱读诗书的青年张某因家境贫困，无法进京赴考，只能在家苦读诗书。张某热情好客，请乾隆皇帝吃顿便饭。正当准备做饭时，张某发现米缸里的米不够吃，又没有菜肴，张某灵机一动，计上心来，叫其妻先准备开火，自己从后门出去到菜园里摘来一把碧绿幼嫩的芥菜，加点佐料，煮成一锅绿中加白的芥菜饭。乾隆皇帝平时吃惯了山珍海味、生猛海鲜，且时至晌午，早已饥肠辘辘，一闻到这芳香扑鼻的芥菜饭，食欲大增，吃得津津有味，赞不绝口，连问这绿里加白的饭是怎么做的。张妻道："这叫芥菜饭，吃了不会生疥疮。"这一天，刚好是农历二月初二，二月二吃芥菜饭的习俗便从此传了下来。

芥菜饭的做法大致如下：选几棵芥菜，洗净，晾干，以免烧芥菜饭时水分含量过高；把要准备煮的糯米先用水浸泡；点火做饭时，先把芥菜切碎，放到锅里爆炒，大约三分钟，可以倒入热开水（冷水亦可）；等水沸腾之后，放进准备好的糯米以及需要的调料，如黄酒、味精等；再盖上锅盖煮大约30分钟，香喷喷的芥菜饭就做好了。

芥菜饭色香味美，深受人们喜爱。在乐清，吃

steamed with the rice and added some condiments. The Emperor was used to the royal feasts and felt extremely hungry when midday came. Once his nose caught the delicious smell of the leaf mustard rice, he fell in love with it and enjoyed it very much. When he asked for the name of the rice, Mr. Zhang's wife answered, "It is leaf mustard rice, it can prevent the scabies." The day happened to be February 2nd, so the custom of eating leaf mustard rice on this day is observed and passed down.

To make the leaf mustard rice one should follow these steps: firstly, wash the picked mustards and dry them in the air in case there is too much water in the mustards when steaming them with rice; the sticky rice is soaked in water before cooked; when the stove is ready, the mustards are chopped and put into the pan for a three-minute quick-fry; then hot boiled water (or cold boiled water) is poured into the pan; after the water is boiling again, the prepared sticky rice and other seasonings such as millet wine and gourmet powder are put into the pan; they have to be boiled for about 30 minutes with the panlid covering on before the delicious leaf mustard rice is finally ready to eat.

Leaf mustard rice is pleasant to both eyes and tongues and becomes one of people's favorites.

In Leqing, this festival practice has been enrolled among the third group of representatives on the Non-material Heritage List. In August, 2003, in a public appraisal sponsored by *Wenzhou Daily*, the practice of "eating leaf mustard rice on February 2nd" is highly recognized by the public and ranked among the Ten Folk Customs in Wenzhou. Nowadays, people enjoy the leaf mustard rice not only on February 2nd, as a healthy diet, the fried rice with leaf mustards, like fried rice with eggs, becomes a common dish in people's daily life.

7.Rice in the Open Air

In Ningbo, Zhejiang Province, it is a popular custom to eat rice in the open air. According to *Chronicles of Ningbo City*, "People eat rice in the open air in February; in the past, on the second day of this month, women would take rice and cookers to

芥菜饭习俗被列入乐清市第三批非物质文化遗产名录。2003年8月，在《温州日报》组织的评选活动中，"二月二吃芥菜饭"这一习俗受到民众热捧，排名高居"温州十大民俗"之列。现在，吃芥菜饭早已不仅仅限于二月初二那一天，作为一种健康蔬菜，芥菜炒饭几乎像蛋炒饭一样成为老百姓经常食用的一道佳肴。

七、露天米饭

在浙江省宁波地区，农历二月初二这天流行吃露天米饭的习俗。根据《宁波市志》记载："二月吃露天米饭，二月初二日，旧时女子相聚携米和炊具去郊外，搭起火灶烧饭，还会偷割农家田园的菜煮羹，俗称'二月二吃露天米饭'，谓吃后人会聪明，乡间称吃'天野羹'。在未吃前，先盛一些饭放在或抛在屋瓦上，让麻雀吃，叫麻雀捎信给百花娘子，祈求灵聪。"

八、多打

山东成武、定陶等地，人们在二月二要吃"多打"。"多打"是由豆子、小米拉成糁子（有半粒米那么大），加上葱姜油盐弄成圆形或扁圆形，上锅蒸成。蒸好之后，年龄大些的老太太用篮子提着或用大襟的衣服兜着，去打谷场转三圈以敬"多打神"，并不断地抠下一点扔在地下，口中念念有词："多打多打多打神，多打粮食多养人；多打多打多打仙，场里麦子堆成山；多打多打多打粮，粮食多了不心慌。"

suburban areas and set up a pot for cooking; sometimes they would even take some vegetables from the nearby farms, it is said that eating rice in the open air on February 2nd will make people wise and quick-witted. In the countryside, it is called 'dinner between sky and field. Before eating, rice are carried on or thrown to tiles on top of the house, which are offered to sparrows to eat. It is hoped that the sparrows will send message for girls to Lady Flower, asking for her blessings to make the girls smart and nimble."

8.Duoda (Getting More)

In Chengwu and Dingtao of Shandong Province, people eat a special food called "Duoda" on February 2nd. Duoda is made of the mixed particles of beans and millets, the size of which is about half of a grain. It is made into the round or oval shape and steamed with green onions, gingers, oil and salts. After Duoda is ready, an old woman of the family would carry it in basket or the front cloth of their dress to the threshing ground and walk around it for three rounds to show respect to the God of Duoda, with every few steps, she would scrabble off some pieces and throw them on the ground while chanting, "I pray to you, God of Duoda, bless us with more food to support the family; I pray to you, God of Duoda, make the wheat in my field piled up like hills; I pray for more grains, the more grains the happier I will be."

9. Steaming a Hill of Chinese Dates

"Steaming a hill of Chinese Dates" is a traditional practice in Longdong region. The "hill of Chinese Dates" is made of a spiraled dough string, whose diameter is about 3 centimeters; the rings it formed all connected with each other, with certain numbers of red dates inlaid (from the upper ring to the bottom ring, the number of red dates are one, three, six, nine, and so on). The "Hill of Chinese Dates" should be made into a shape of human being, the head is oval-shaped, the five sense organs on the face are made by black beans, arms and legs are made of cylinder-like dough; it is supported by two red chopsticks on the back so that it can stand steadily. On February 2nd, housewives put the "Hill of Chinese Dates" in the field, and the whole family would scrabble some pieces off the "hill" and spread them in the field for praying after they have worshipped the God of Earth, and then they share the "Hill of Chinese Dates" together before the master of the house ploughing a patch of the field, which, according to the proverb "on February 2nd when dragon raises its head, the granaries are filled and the harvest is coming", will promise favorable weather free from natural disasters such as flood, hail and frost, and a harvest year with all granaries filled with grains.

九、蒸枣山

"蒸枣山"是陇东地区的重要习俗。"枣山"用直径约3厘米的面花旋成，环环相扣，每环嵌一定数目的红枣（一三六九排列）。"枣山"要做成人形，头部呈椭圆状，五官用黑豆镶嵌，胳膊、腿用圆柱形面杠做成，背后由两根红筷子支撑，以便立放。二月二日，家庭主妇将"枣山"送到地头，全家先拜土地神，再拧下几块撒祭、祈祷，并在地头分吃"枣山"，而后还要由户主套犁耕一段地，以合"二月二，龙抬头，大仓满，小仓流"的俗谚。俗信这样就可保证一年之内不遭洪涝雹霜等自然灾害，可以保证一年之内风调雨顺、五谷丰登、粮堆如山。

十、做"圣虫"

在山东的胶东地区，有春节、二月二做"圣虫"的民俗。所谓"圣虫"，就是传统面食，一般做成龙、蛇、刺猬或虎面蛇身等形状。二月二是龙抬头的日子，这期间的"圣虫"以龙形象为主。做"圣虫"，先用面揉成龙状，再用剪刀在面团上轻轻剪几下，剪出一排排的龙鳞，然后用豆子点睛，放到锅里蒸熟，一条活生生的"龙"便出现了。"圣虫"形象各异，或威风凛凛，或活泼可爱，且有公母之分，浑身剪出龙鳞的是公的，没有龙鳞的则是母的。

"圣虫"做好后，一般被放置在粮仓或面缸里面，当地人相信米缸里放了"圣虫"，米面不生虫子，而且"圣虫"还包含着美好的寓意。"圣"与"生""升""剩"等谐音，意为"生粮""剩粮"，寓意五谷丰登，越吃越有。"圣虫"的摆放很讲究，摆在面缸

10. Making the "Holy Animals"

In Jiaodong District of Shandong Province, it is the local common practice to make "holy animals" on Spring Festival and February 2nd. "Holy animals" refer to the traditional foods made of flour that are made into the shape of dragons, snakes, hedgehogs and beasts with tiger's face and snake's body. February 2nd is the day when dragons raise their heads, thus most of the "holy animals" made on this day are in the shape similar to dragons. When making a holy animal, people often knead the dough into the shape of dragon and cut out lines of dragon scales on the dough with scissors. Beans are placed on the dragon's head as eyes. The finished dragon-shape dough is then put into pot to be boiled and steamed before a lively "dragon" appears. The holy animals have different looks: some are majestic-looking and some are lively and lovable. There are male and female ones, the former having scales on them and the latter having none.

When the "holy animals" are finished, they are put into granaries and flour vats as local people believe that rice and flour won't be eaten by worms or insects with "holy animals" in their containers. The name of "holy animals" is also of good connotation. The pronunciation of "holy" is homophonous to that of "birth", "rise" and "rich" in Chinese pinyin, which means more food, abundant harvest and greater prosperity. The place to put holy animals should be carefully chosen, for example, female ones are often put in flour vats as it is believed that female "holy animals" can bring more food to the family.

Making "holy animals" is a display of Shandong people's passion for future life. There is a beautiful story about the origin of "holy animals". Once upon a time, a rich family was holding a wedding in the winter. On the way to the bridegroom's house, the bride found a worm nearly freezing to death. She was so sympathetic about it that she held it in her arms to get it warmed up. The eight men carrying the sedan felt that the weight on their shoulders was increasing and they were all tired out when they reached the destination. The bride was worried about the dying worm hidden in her sleeves when she was greeted in the wedding house. She asked her mother-in-law where the family granary was. The mother was happy to see that her daughter-in-law was ready to get familiar with the housework, so she showed the bride around the granaries in the house. The bride took the chance and put the worm in one of the granaries. Later, the village met a famine, the bride persuaded her mother-in-law to open the granaries to the hungry villagers. They could take as much rice as they wanted in the rich family's granaries. As a result, the whole village was saved. Three days later, the bride came to the granaries with her mother-in-law. To their surprise, the food in the granaries was still there without any difference in quantity. It turned out that the worm saved by the bride was a holy animal. To return her favor,

里的"圣虫"最好选母的，因为母的"圣虫"能生，放在里面才越吃越有。

做"圣虫"寄寓了胶东人民对美好生活的憧憬。关于"圣虫"的来历，在山东莱州地区流传着一个美丽的传说：从前，有一户富裕的人家在寒冬腊月娶亲。在迎亲回来的路上，新娘子看到路上躺着一只冻得哆哆嗦嗦的虫子，觉得它可怜，便把它抱起来藏在怀里取暖。抬轿的八个壮汉感觉轿子越来越沉，左肩换右肩，好不容易才把它抬到新郎家。众人喜气洋洋地把新媳妇迎进新房，而新娘却惦记着怀里的虫子，忙问婆婆粮囤在哪儿。婆婆一听心里十分欢喜，认为新媳妇能持家、会过日子，就领着媳妇挨个粮囤转了一圈，新媳妇趁机把虫放到粮囤里。后来这村子闹了饥荒，新媳妇劝说婆婆开仓三天，救济全村，让村民到粮仓取粮食，能取多少取多少。因此，全村人都得救了。三天后，新媳妇领着婆婆到粮仓一看，粮囤里的粮食丝毫未减。原来，新媳妇救了一只神虫，它为了报答救命之恩，把粮囤又给填满了。从此，人们为了纪念神虫，也为了祈愿五谷丰登、风调雨顺，每逢新婚、春节等喜庆日子，都要用面粉做成神虫的样子放在粮囤里供奉，并称其为"圣虫"。

the worm fulfilled the granaries of the family. Since then people began to make dough into the shape of holy animals in memory of the holy worm and to pray for a good harvest and favorable weather. On the occasion of wedding days and spring festivals, people make holy animals and enshrine them in the granaries; that's how the name of "holy animals" come into being.

3 二月二，接宝贝儿
Coming home

在中国，许多地方二月二是亲戚邻居，特别是姻亲之间礼尚往来的特定时间。其中，接出嫁的女儿回娘家是相当普遍的做法。俗话说"二月二，

In many places of China, February 2nd is a special time for neighbors and families tied with marriage relationships to visit each other. It is a common practice to greet their married daughters at home, as a saying goes like this, "Girls are coming home on the second day of February, otherwise the parents are left heartbroken", which means if a girl fails to visit her parents on that day, the parents will shed tear for her absence. Another saying also describes this occasion, "On February 2nd when dragon raises its head, parents greet their home-coming daughters and listen to their complaints about marriage and life." It is implied that in a society where the husband dominates in the family, the wife's visiting her parents at times will help to release her homesickness and pressure, and also strengthen the relationship between the husband's parental family and the wife's. On February 2nd, temple fairs all over the country greet large crowds of people, which becomes a common practice for relatives to keep in touch with each other. People often take this occasion to visit the relatives who live near the temple fair, and the host will prepare a delicious dinner with good wine to entertain the guests. Such an emotional communication between relatives is conducted regularly thanks to the festival. In addition, people take out the seasoned beans, pancakes and sugar puddings to their neighbors on the Day of February 2nd. The gift sending activities help to build up a friendly, mutual-benefited atmosphere in the community.

1.Married Daughters' Coming Home

February 2nd marks the beginning of a busy farming season. It is the day when married daughters

接宝贝儿，接不来，掉眼泪儿"，意思就是闺女不回来，娘家爹妈就会伤感而泣。另一句俗谚是"二月二龙抬头，家家接女诉冤愁"，说明在从夫居的社会里，回娘家有助于疏通女子因异处生活而积聚的对娘家人的思念，强化婆家与娘家之间的关系。二月二日，全国各地庙会众多，逛庙会、走亲戚成为许多地区的一种亲戚往来的常态。人们往往利用庙会时机，到庙会所在地的亲戚家拜访一番，而主家则要提前准备，好酒好饭款待，亲戚之间的情感交流借助二月二节日得以定期展开。另外，二月二期间，人们会把自家炒的料豆、摊的煎饼、炸的糖糕送给邻居品尝，这种节日期间互相馈赠礼物的行为，能够建立、维护和强化社区内邻里间的互惠友好关系。

一、回娘家

二月二的到来，意味着即将进入农忙时节。这一天，全国普遍流行接出嫁的闺女回娘家过节，人们希望利用农忙前最后的闲暇时光，与已嫁的闺女团聚一下。

回娘家是出嫁女子对原有生活空间和社会网络的回归，是一种心灵的回归和情感的重温。倘若前一阵在婆家受了气，或遇到不顺之事，借二月二回到娘家诉说一番，心里自然就轻松通畅许多。同时，它还是外甥与舅家确认和强化关系的方式，是对姻亲关系的一种定期维护、强化和刷新。比如在河北赵县，二月二娘家人去接女儿时，要顺便送给

return to their parents' houses for a reunion holiday as they cherish the last leisure moment before the busy farming time.

Coming home is a spiritual return and an emotional revisit to the married girl's earlier life space and her old social network. If she has trouble with the husband's family, or meets something disagreeable in life, she can look for comfort from her parental family on the home coming occasion and become cheerful again. Meanwhile, it is also a way to strengthen the relationship between the nephews and uncles and to maintain and refresh the marriage bonds between two families involved. In Zhao County, Hebei Province, when the girl's family sends for the daughter, they would bring some gifts to the husband's family; and when the daughter return from her parents' house, she would

bring back some carps and pork to her mother-in-law to show her respect, which is called "resuming a meat diet".

It is notable that though in most regions, it is a custom for married girls to visit their parents, it is prohibited in some places, as it is believed if the married daughters go back to her parental house on that day, they will bring misfortune or even death to the husband's brothers or parents. This taboo balances social relations in an unusual way. If going back to the parents' house is to find a balance for the married women with her life and social relations before marriage, on the contrary, not going back home on this special day serves as an emphasis on her belonging to the new life and social relations after marriage.

2. Getting in Touch With Relatives

There are a large number of temple fairs all over the country on February 2nd, while the married daughters return to their parents' houses. People

女儿婆家一些礼物，等到女儿再回婆家时，还要备好鲤鱼和猪肉送给婆婆以示孝敬，俗称"开素"。

值得注意的是，虽然多数地方强调二月二出嫁的女子要回娘家，但在有些地方则格外禁止这一行为，并有"吃了娘家花，死老大伯全家"、"吃了娘家虫，回家搭灵篷"、"过了二月二，回家死小叔"、"二月二踩了娘家的仓，不死公爹就死婆婆娘"等说法。这一禁忌，其实也是对既有社会关系的一种调谐，只不过采取了另外一种方式。如果说，二月二让女子回娘家，更多的是要协调女子与出嫁前原有的生活空间、社会网络的连带关系，那么二月二不让女子回娘家，则是在这一特定的节日期间，格外强调女子与出嫁后新有的生活空间、社会网络的归属关系。

二、走亲戚

全国各地二月二日有很多庙会，这一天除了闺女回娘家，人们也都会趁着赶庙会的时机去走亲戚。因此，庙会附近的几个村子，每家每户在二月初一前就会精心准备饭菜，招待二月二来做客的亲戚朋友。

甘肃省岷县秦许乡包家族村每年都有二月二庙会，庙会期间是这个小山村一年中最热闹的时刻，比过年还要热闹许多。届时，会有几万人拥入这个人口只有一千多的小村庄，每家每户来客爆满，村民要不断地迎来送往，热情招待如潮水般涌来过节的客人。男人通常是陪客人聊天、喝茶、

also visit the relatives on this occasion. Therefore, villages near the temple fairs will prepare dinners before February 1st to entertain the visiting relatives and friends on the very day.

In Min County, Gansu Province, Temple Fair on February 2nd is held every year, which is the busiest and most bustling time in this small mountain village, even more exciting than the Spring Festival. On this occasion, millions of people swarm into this small village whose population is merely more than one thousand; every house is crowded with guests and the hosts are busy with receptions. Men chat with guests over a cup of tea and have dinners with them, while women are in charge of all housework. For women of the Bao people, "February 2nd" is a busy festival. In fact, women are preparing for this

day ever since the last ten days in January. The first thing to do is a general cleaning, especially washing the beddings, as when the festival day comes, there will be a lot of relatives and friends coming to stay, which means clean bed sheets and quilt covers are needed. The next thing are festival foods, most of which are bean-made, such as dried and fried beans and bean sprouts. When relatives come, the bean-made foods are cooked with bacon to entertain the guests. On the 28th day of January, the housewives steam several cauldrons of steamed buns; on 29th they make bean jelly, and on 30th they stew bones and meats. Relatives and friends begin to arrive since January 30th, which is time to test the women's labor results. Every house is filled with guests and the hosts provide three meals a day and are considerate enough to make them as comfortable as in their own houses. Guests come and go in groups, and it is the housewives who are in charge of cooking, washing the dishes and cleaning the rooms all day long, which is a tiring but proud job, as they believe it is the most glorious moment for the Bao people, which is a fame people in town can't be awarded.

吃饭，女人则要做好一切后勤工作。对于包家族妇女来说，"二月二"实在是个忙碌的节日。其实，妇女们从正月下旬就开始为过二月二做准备了。最早进行的准备工作是大扫除，尤其是床上用品的洗涤。因为过会期间家里可能要有好多亲戚朋友前来住宿，所以要提前洗干净床单、被套。接下来就是要准备节日期间的食品，以豆制品居多，如烘炒的豆子、水生的豆芽。亲戚来了，就把这些豆菜加上腊肉炒成美味，供客人享用。从正月二十八开始，主妇要蒸上几锅馍馍，正月二十九做凉粉，正月三十煮好骨头、肉。从正月三十这天开始，来过"二月二"节的亲戚朋友就会陆续驾临。这意味着包家族妇女的劳动成果接受检验的时刻到了。每家客人都很多，主人家要一日三餐好好招待，不敢怠慢。有时候是这批客人刚吃完，另一批客人接着吃，家里主妇所要做的工作就是不停地做饭、洗碗、打扫卫生等，很是劳累。但是，她们心里甚感自豪，认为这是包家族人最风光的时刻，比城里人都要风光。

二月二期间，类似包家族的村落数不胜数。借助庙会，单纯的嫁女归宁习俗就逐渐演变成了更为宽泛的亲朋相聚，这种氛围下的二月二节在当地显得格外热闹。

当然，二月二调谐的还不止是基于血缘和姻缘形成的亲属关系，还形塑着基于地缘而形成的社会关系。在许多地方，虽然家家都会摊煎饼，或者炸糖糕，或者炒麦豆，但还是要把自制饮食送给别人家品尝，社区居民之间互相馈赠节礼的交际圈由此形成。礼尚往来之际，固然有借助他人力量以求得农业丰产、生活康宁的仪式性设想（如大家一起遵从节俗以驱虫避害），但更重要的是借此建立、维护和强化彼此之间互助互惠的友好关系，感受人际温情，创造生活滋味。

A variety of villages follow such a practice like the Bao people on February 2nd. Thanks to the temple fairs, the practice of married girls returning home becomes a family reunion of relatives and friends, which makes the Day of February 2nd more warm and exciting among local people.

Of course, February 2nd not only harmonizes the kinship based on blood ties and marriage ties, but also shapes the social relationship based on geography. In many places, though all households make pancakes, fried sweet cakes and fried wheat beans, they take out the home-made foods to their neighbors, thus a social network is formed among community members by sending gifts. As an old custom of "courtesy meets reciprocity", this practice, on the one hand, becomes a ritual followed by people to gain a harvest and a peaceful and healthy life with the help of others (for example, everyone observes the practice of getting rid of bad insects); on the other hand, it is an effort to build, maintain and strengthen a friendly and mutually beneficial relationship, and an approach to the best part of human relations and the essence of life.

4 二月二，逛庙会
Visiting Temple Fairs

"On February 2nd, people put aside their farm work and enjoy the pancake", the saying gives a lively description of the festival atmosphere where people are in mood for fun. Everyone is looking forward to a good relaxation at the end of the Spring Festival to prepare themselves for the new round of hard work. Therefore, many things are forbidden to do on February 2nd in many places, for instance, people are not allowed to do needle work, neither using knives and scissors nor using the grind, etc. All of these taboos make the day a true time for rest and entertainment in every sense, which is so precious to women who deal with needles and scissors all day long. For a whole day on February 2nd, there is no need to work, and women have plenty of time to enjoy themselves: visiting her parents with her children, shopping in temple fairs and going for spring outing in the fields. For children, the day is one of the happiest moments

"二月二，不干活，坐下来，吃大馍"，这句俗语生动地道出了二月二在人们心目中的休闲、娱乐色彩。人们要利用这年节的尾巴，好好放松一下身心，以应付接下来一年的农耕劳作。正因如此，许多地方的二月二都有若干禁忌，如不能动针线，不能用刀剪，不能用磨等。所有禁忌，使得二月二成为一个合法的休闲时间，这对于整日与针线刀剪打交道的传统女性而言何其珍贵！二月二整整一天，她们无活一身轻，可以带着孩子回娘家，可以去逛庙会，可以去野外踏青。而对于孩子而言，二月二更是快乐时光，许多节俗活动都允许他们参与其中。孩子们可以在大人打灰囤时高兴地跑来跑去，可以在仓囤里埋粮食，可以唱着歌谣围着墙根撒灰，可以拿着炒豆、爆玉米花与同伴交换、攀比、斗赛。可以说，二月二诸多节俗的设置，为乡村的男女老少提供了一个宽广的休闲空间。

一、赶庙会

二月二，赶庙会至少在明代已经出现，清朝、民国期间十分盛行。20世纪中叶到20世纪80年代以前衰落。近年来，随着国家非物质文化遗产保护运动的持续升温，二月二庙会大有复兴之势。

在我国北方地区，二月二常常与庙会联系在一起，赶庙会是许多地方二月二的常规活动，而南方地区也有少量的庙会活动。

二月二庙会往往具有多重性质，或是以信仰为主的香火会，或是以物

in their lives, as they are allowed to take part in a variety of festival activities; they run and jump around when adults draw the granary on the ground, hide grains in the barns and sing the ballads when spreading ash along the walls; they can exchange fried beans and popcorns with their friends, comparing and competing with each other for the best tasted snacks. All of these activities provide great fun to people of all ages in the countryside.

1.Going to Temple Fairs

Going to Temple Fair on February 2nd made its early appearance in Ming Dynasty, and became popular in late Qing Period and Republican Period. It suffered from a decline during 1950s to 1980s. In recent years, with the development of the national campaign of protecting non-material cultural heritage, Temple Fairs on February 2nd is on its way to revival.

In North China, February 2nd is often related to temple fairs, which form the major practice on that day in many places; but it is seldom observed in South China.

Temple Fair on February 2nd has many themes, some of them are worshipping ceremony based on religious beliefs, and some of them are trading

fairs based on material exchanging. No matter what kind of fairs they are, there are always gorgeous performances. In Qinxu Village of Min County in Gansu, opera performances will last for three days, and there are a number of games to play, such as ring-throwing, frog-games, points-guessing, lottery, shooting balloons and kite-flying; in Bailongbu of Pizhou in Jiangsu, there are all kinds of performances, such as Lahun Opera, Lotus Rhyme, Yu Drum Chanting, story-telling, stilt -walking, boat dancing and lion dancing; on the god worshipping temple fairs in Huangtian of Hezhou in Guangxi , festival activities include dragon dancing, lion dancing, operas and firework-grabbing, and acrobatics are performed by folk artists from Yao people, which include climbing ladders of swords, burning body with incenses and walking through

质交流为主的买卖会。不管哪种庙会，都不免有炫人耳目的景象呈现。如甘肃岷县秦许乡的二月二庙会，必唱三天四夜大戏，庙会上有套圈、青蛙游戏、押大小点、摇奖、枪打气球、放风筝等各种好玩的游戏；在江苏邳州白龙埠的二月二庙会上，曾有唱拉魂腔、说莲花落、唱渔鼓、说评书、走高跷、跑旱船、耍狮子等各种表演异彩纷呈；在广西贺州黄田的二月二祀神庙会上，既有舞龙、舞狮、唱戏、抢炮等活动，又有瑶族人表演上刀山、过刀梯、香火烧身、过火炼等民间绝技；在山西省平顺县的豆口二月二庙会上，有扭秧歌、踩高跷、表演拳术、骑竹马、跑旱船、耍龙灯、栓高台等数十种民间文艺节目，等等。人在庙会中，目之所睹，耳之所闻，身之所触，乃至鼻之所嗅、舌之所品，无不异于常日。所有这些，都为身处其中的民众带来了莫大享受。

二、踏青、迎富、挑菜

农历二月二日，北方虽然仍然寒冷，但已有春意，加上禁止劳作是普遍的节俗，因此呼朋引伴、携子带女到郊外踏青不失为一项惬意的活动。二月二踏青、迎富、挑菜等在唐宋时期就已存在的习俗，至今仍在河北、山西、浙江、河南、陕西、四川等地有所流行。

二月二放风筝、挑菜、迎富等活动，在山西、陕西、河南一带早

fires; on Doukou Temple Fair, there are dozens of folk art performances, such as yangko dancing, stilt walking, Chinese boxing, hobbyhorse riding, boat dancing, dragon lantern dancing and high-stage-performance. On temple fairs, everything is felt so different from the ordinary daily life, which is a refreshing experience to the senses of eyes, ears, body, nose and tongue, and brings happiness and enjoyment to people involved in.

2.Spring outing, Greeting God of Wealth and Picking up Vegetables

On Lunar February 2nd, though it is still cold in North China, the coming spring brings warmth to people's life; as the festival practice discourage working on the very day, the best way to enjoy the spring is going out in the outskirts and fields with friends and children. Spring outing, Wealth God greeting and picking up vegetables on February 2nd were common practice dating back to Tang and Song Dynasties, and they are still observed in Hebei, Shanxi, Zhejiang, Henan, Shaanxi and Sichuan.

Flying kites, picking up vegetables and greeting the God of Wealth on February 2nd have long been popular in Shanxi, Shaanxi and Henan. In Xinjiang,

Shanxi Province, girls enjoy spring outing and small kids are fond of flying kites. In Yichuan, Shaanxi Province, women go to the fields to pick up vegetables with friends on that day. In Huayin, people go to outskirts in the morning and return at sunset, marching along the road beating drums and blowing trumpets, which are called "greeting the God of Wealth".

3.Praying for Light Hands

In villages of Cizhou, Hebei Province, girls often pray for light hands on February 2nd. On this day, girls put on new clothes and go cooking on the hills; they bring pots and bowls along with them as well as fuel, rice, cooking oil and salt; the things they cook include millet rice, dumplings and porridge. When the meals are ready, everyone would go

有流传。在山西新绛，女子踏青，小儿放风筝，以为笑乐。在陕西宜川，这天妇女时兴呼朋引伴往郊外觅野菜。华阴一带民众携鼓乐到郊外去，朝往暮回，沿路吹吹打打，名为"迎富"。

三、乞巧、做乞巧饭

在河北磁州山村里，姑娘们有在二月二乞巧的习俗。这天，姑娘们穿上新衣裳，自带锅碗以及柴米油盐，在山上支锅做饭，如焖小米饭、包水饺、煮米粥等。饭熟后，每人去摘七个圪针尖，然后乞巧。乞巧的规则是这样的：

姑娘们按照乞巧的仪式，先把一个姑娘的眼睛用布捂起来，叫她把手里的七个圪针尖儿撒在饭锅里，再递给她一双筷子，在饭锅里轻轻搅上三搅，然后就用筷子夹起饭来吃。只准吃七口，要能吃到七个圪针尖儿，就会成为心灵手巧的姑娘。一个姑娘吃过了，再将另一个姑娘的眼捂起，在锅里补足七个圪针尖儿，用筷子搅上三搅，然后一口一口地吃七口，依次挨下去。最后她们会排出次序来，凡是吃到七个圪针尖儿的，大家就称她为巧姐或巧妹，会受到同伴们的爱戴和尊敬。[1]

四、打尜童戏

山东各地盛行二月二日打尜的游戏。打尜，有的地区叫打尖、打茧、打

---

[1] 王永信等主编：《赵都民俗趣话》，北京：中国民间文艺出版社，1989年，第9页。

around looking for seven kudzu needles and begin the ritual of praying for light hands, which goes like this:

According to the rituals of praying for light hands, one of the girls covers her eyes with a piece of cloth, and spreads her seven kudzu needles into the rice pot; a pair of chopsticks is handed over to her, with which she stirs in the pot three times and then fetches the rice into her mouth; only seven mouthfuls are allowed, and if the needles are hidden in one of the mouthfuls she eats, she is blessed to be the girl with a pair of light hands. The girls follow these steps one by one, dropping her needles into the pot, stirring and eating seven mouthfuls. After this, they count the numbers of needles they get during this process, the girl who gets all of the seven needles she drops in the pot is called Sister Qiao (the clever girl) and is admired among her friends.[1]

4.Children's Game: Striking the Ga (a toy pointed at two ends)

The game of striking the *Ga* is very popular in Shandong, which is called "striking the spinning top", "striking the cocoon" or "striking Lazi" in

---

[1] Edited by Wang Yongxin, etc. *Funny Folklore Stories of the Ancient Capital of Zhao*. Chinese Folk Literature and Art Publishing House, 1989, p. 9

some places. The game has a long history, according to *Sceneries and Customs in the Capital* by Liu Tong, "On February 2nd when dragon raises its head, children get a wooden piece of about two cun (1/3 decimeter) in the shape of date pit and drop it on the ground; they hit it with a club as far as possible, the one who doesn't hit it far enough is considered the loser. They play this game every day, which is also called hitting the ground." The piece they hit in the above description looks like a date pit, which is similar to the *ga*. In *Chronicles of Laiyang County* of 1935, "Children divide themselves into groups and draw circle on the ground; they cut a wooden piece of about one cun long with the two ends pointed, and hit it by a batten, which is called striking the spinning top; they put up a piece of

拉子等。这项活动历史颇为悠久，据刘侗《帝京景物略》记载："二月二日龙抬头，小儿以木二寸制如枣核，置地而棒之，一击令起，随一击令远，以近者为负，日打柭（梯）柭，古所称击壤者耶！"书中的柭形如枣核，两头尖，中间大，与现在的岁相差无几。民国二十四年《莱阳县志》记载："群儿党分，画地为锅，削木寸余，锐其两端，以板击之，谓之'打尖'。因竖板于锅，还掷中板则胜，

否则负。"打尜游戏，取材简单，玩法多样，因而在境内广泛流行，至今仍十分盛行，只不过早已不再局限于二月二节俗期间进行了。

batten inside the circle on the ground, and try to hit the batten with the piece of wood, those who hit it by striking the piece are the winners." The game props are simple and easy to make, the patterns of playing are variable, therefore, the game is popular among the children all over the area till today, and it is no longer played exclusively on February 2nd, but is played whenever one likes.

第三章

二月二的各地异俗

　　我国领土广袤，文明悠久，"二月二"节俗南北差异明显，并因文化传播和民族融合而形成比较复杂的态势。比如在节日信仰方面，南方是信仰土地神，北方则普遍流行崇拜龙神。大致说来，南方地区山多、江河多而土地少，自上古以来人们敬土为神，其祭社习俗一直传袭至今，演变成"二月二"的社日习俗。北方大部分地区长年干旱少雨，地表水源短缺，而农作物的生长又离不开水，人们渴盼多水、期待降雨的心理可谓强烈，这不仅表现在"二月二"节俗中的"引龙"、"食龙"等家庭活动之中，而且借助整个社区的"酬龙"、"龙牌会"等庙会活动予以表达。但无论如何，祈福禳灾以求风调雨顺、五谷丰登，则是二月二节俗中的永恒主题。

Chapter Three
Customs on February 2nd

As China boasts a wast land and a time-honored civilization, distinctive differences exist in celebrating February 2nd between its north and south parts and grow more complicated for its cultural communication and national integration. For instance, in terms of festival worship, southerners believe in the God of Earth, while northerners worship the God of Dragon. Generally speaking, there are more mountains and hills than rivers and lands in the southern areas since the ancient times, thus people worship the earth as their god and the practice is passed down by generations and finally become the custom of celebrating the Earth Day on February 2nd nowadays. Most of the northern areas, however, are arid inlands with rare rainfall and a shortage of surface water. As water plays an essential role in the growth of crops, people in these areas all have a strong desire for rainfalls, which is reflected in family activities such as "inviting dragons" and "dragon food" when celebrating February 2nd, and is expressed through community activities such as "rewarding dragons" and "dragon tablet club". Despite all these differences, the timeless theme of celebrating February 2nd has always been praying for god's blessings and asking for nice weather as well as a good harvest.

1

京西 "酬龙节"
The Day of Rewarding the Dragons in the West of Beijing

A river runs through Fangshan District of the southwest of Beijing, along which the Town of Hebei, the Town of Fozizhuang and Nanjiao Village form the famous Hetao Channel District. There is a well-known temple in this area, which is called Temple of the God of Dragon in Black Dragon Pass. Every year on February 2nd, local people hold a grand temple fair to worship the gods. This is the so-called "February Temple Fairs". A series of rules and rituals take shape after so many years of worshipping.

北京市西南的房山区，有一条大石河穿境而过，沿岸的河北镇、佛子庄乡、南窖乡一带就是有名的"河套沟"地区。这里有一座远近闻名的庙宇——黑龙关龙神庙，每年的二月二日，当地民众都会自发组织盛大的庙会活动，俗称"二月庙"。在长期进香活动中，他们产生了独具特色的组织和仪式。

一、黑龙庙与黑龙潭

因龙神庙坐落于此，佛子庄乡的黑龙关村自然成为庙会活动的中心。这个美丽的山村紧傍大石河，附近山陡涧深，聚落呈带状，如一艘大船，两头尖，中间宽。村北有一片长七八百米、宽约一百米的大石河水域，便是黑龙潭。黑龙关龙神庙坐落在黑龙潭上的绝涧上，它三面环山，一面悬崖临大石河，是京西重要的求雨中心。

1. The Temple of Black Dragon and the Lake of Black Dragon

The Temple of the God of Dragon is seated in the Black Dragon Pass Village of the Town of Fozizhuang, which becomes the center of the temple fairs activities. The beautiful village stands close to the River of Big Stone, with steep mountains and deep creeks nearby, and the layout of the village is like a huge ship with tow pointed and body in the middle wide. In the north of the village, there is a water area of 700 to 800 meters long and about 100 meters wide, this is the Lake of Black Dragon. The Temple of God of Dragon lies on the lake, surrounded by mountains on three sides, the cliff of the fourth side facing the River of Big Stone; it is an important spot for people in the west of Beijing praying for rain.

The Temple of the God of Dragon faces the south with a three-section compound structure, the two sides of which are surrounded by mountains. The three major rooms stand near the cliffs of the mountains, with two guarding rooms on their sides, one on the east and the other the west; the courtyard is surrounded by red walls, inside are four cypress trees of about 300 years old. The gate of the courtyard faces the Black Dragon Pass Village, with a screen wall in front of it, overlooking the Lake of Black Dragon below. The God of Dragon and the Goddess of Dragon are enshrined and worshipped in the major hall; on the side of the couple stands ten gods, the five on the east are: the God of Day, the God of Accounting, the God of Ruler, the God of Rain and the God of Thunder; the five on the west are: the God of Courtyard, the God of Wind, the God of Umbrella, the God of Lightening and the God of Heaven. The ten gods vary in their facial expressions, each with a treasure in their hands, such as umbrella, ruler, bag of winds, account book, thunder hammer and lightening devices, which are said to be necessary when making the rain. On the wall of the major hall, five frescos are painted, telling the story of the God of the Dragon working for the Jia family of Zhaitang in Mentou Channel District. In front of the hall, there is an inscribed board written by Emperor Yongzheng of Qing Dynasty, reading "the rain in time benefits the world"; later his son, Emperor Qianlong wrote an antithetical couplet reading: "conquering the oceans and relieving people from their sufferings, the contribution is more

龙神庙坐北朝南，为三合院结构，左右皆山，靠山崖有正殿三间，东西配殿各一间，四周是红色围墙。院内植有四株侧柏，树龄在300年左右。其正门正对黑龙关村，门前有一影壁，下临黑龙潭。正殿供奉着龙神爷和龙神奶奶，两侧立有十位天神，东侧的五位是算日子神、记账神、尺神、雨神和雷公，而监院神、风神、伞神、电神和天神则立于正殿西侧。十位天神神态各异，手上分别拿着

伞、尺子、风口袋、账本、雷锤、电具等各色宝物，据说这些都是下雨时要用到的神器。正殿的墙壁上绘有五幅壁画，讲述着龙神爷当年在门头沟斋堂贾家扛长活的故事。正殿前，有清雍正皇帝御笔赐匾"甘泽普应"，后又有乾隆赐联："御四海济苍生，功能配社；驾六龙享庶物，德可参天。"

旧时，每逢五六月的大旱时节，这一带的"六山会"①就会组织花会前往黑龙关龙潭祈雨。届时，四面八方的香客、花会都来此进香并朝拜龙神爷。有求必有报。在求雨后来年的二月初一到初三，黑龙关龙神庙都要举办三天庙会，此时各村花会齐集龙神庙酬神献艺。围绕着求雨和庙会，河套沟一带的花会极

---

① "六山会"是新中国成立之前河套沟一带由村民自发组成的一种联村机构，它独立于村落的行政机构，主要组织求雨、走会等活动，兼管地方治安。组成人员中既有一般的老百姓，又有各村花会的会头、村里的村正等。辐射范围基本涉及了佛子庄乡、南窖乡、河北镇的大部分地区。

---

enormous than the earth; driving six dragons and sharing with all the creatures, the merits are higher than the heaven."

In the past, when the dry season arrived in May and June, the "Six Mountain Club"[1] would send its members to pray for rains in the Lake of Black Dragon, when prayers all over the region came and worshipped the God of Dragon. People reward the god for his kindness after every worship activity. From February 1st to 3rd in the coming year after the rain praying ceremony, people hold a three-day temple fair for a performance to reward the god. The theme temple fair in Hetao Channel District is extremely colorful with dozens of performances, such as lion dancing, flag dancing, drum performing, stilts walking and music concert. Today, the old

---

[1]Six Mountain Club is an organization spontaneously established among villagers before 1949 to handle village affairs. It is independent from the administrative service in the village as it is in charge of activities such as praying for rain and folk arts performances as well as public security. Its members include ordinary villagers, heads of folk arts teams and heads of villages. It influences Fozizhuang Village, Nanjiao Village and the a large area from Hebei Town.

practice of praying for rain fades away, but the "February Temple Fairs" in Black Dragon Pass is maintained and becomes an important event on February 2nd to reward and entertain the dragons.

2. The Day of Rewarding Dragons on February 1st

From March 8th to 9th, 2008, which is February 1st to 2nd in lunar calendar, people from Fozizhuang County held *The Third Folk Arts Performance of Fozizhuang County to celebrate the Day of Rewarding Dragons* in front of the God of Dragon Temple in Black Dragon Pass. Township government started the preparation work since January 8th in lunar calendar. The performances this year include the drum playing from villages of the town and the time-honored "silver voice" concert from Chen village; the well-known huckster Zang Hong was invited to host the performance, and opera troupe of Hebei *bangzi* (one of the Chinese opera) are invited to perform traditional opera repertoires such as *A Sad Story of the Girl Named Dou'e* and *Ascend the Throne*; the aim of the temple fairs is to revive the original folk culture.

On February 1st, the re-decorated Temple

其繁多，有十几档，如狮子会、幡会、大鼓会、高跷会、音乐会等。时至今天，求雨这一古老的习俗已消失在历史长河中，但黑龙关"二月庙"一直延续至今，已经成为当地人们在二月二这天的重要活动，表达着酬龙、娱龙的情感。

二、二月初一：酬龙节

2008年3月8日—9日，阴历二月初一到初二，佛子庄乡在黑龙关龙神庙前举办了"酬龙节暨佛子庄乡第三届民俗花会汇演"。乡政府从正月初八就开始了筹备工作，这年的庙会不仅有乡内各庄的大鼓，号称音乐"活化石"的陈家台村银音会，还特意请来京城著名叫卖大王臧鸿来主持这次活动；更邀请了河北梆子剧团，演唱《窦娥冤》《大登殿》等传统剧目，目的就是要"办一个原生态庙会"。

二月初一这天，装饰

一新的龙神庙已经有了喜庆的气氛。在正殿的三合院里，一头宰杀的生猪被供奉在正殿前。这头黑猪全身光溜溜的，脖子上绑着红布，背上留有一撮黑毛。这是等着晚上给龙神爷敬献的生猪。当地人说，供奉给龙神爷的必须是黑猪，而且要去毛的。旧时庙会只献猪头，而不是一整头猪。村民对此的解释是，当地一直有过二月二吃猪头肉的传统。

中午时分，香客陆续来到庙前，烧香敬神。烧香之后，要到正殿前磕头许愿，因为他们相信"烧香一定要磕头，不磕头等于经白求"。此时，庙里

of the God of Dragon was bathed in the festival atmosphere. In the three-section courtyard, a slaughtered pig was placed in front of the major hall; the black pig was bare with only a piece of red cloth wrapped around its neck and some black hair left on its back; it would be offered to the God of Dragon in the evening. It was said that the sacrifice to the God of Dragon must be a black pig with its hair shaven. In the past, only pig's head was offered on the temple fair instead of a whole pig. Villagers explain it because of the festival practice of eating meat of pig's head on February 2nd.

At noon, prayers came to the temple, burning the incense and worshipping the gods. After that, they came to the major hall to kowtow, as they believed that "burning incense must be followed by kowtowing, or the praying is in vain". At this time, there were not many people in the temple, except the local prayers and some coming from far away. Besides burning the incense and praying, the prayers would try to "press coins" on the stone tablet in front of the hall; it was said that anyone who could make the coins stay steadily on the tablet would be blessed by the Dragon God.[1] With the hope of good fortune, people all pressed the coins arduously on the tablet and wished that the moment they loosened the grip, the coin would stay firmly on the tablet as if pasted by all-purpose adhesive. The tablet does have several coins staying on it for a long time without dropping off.

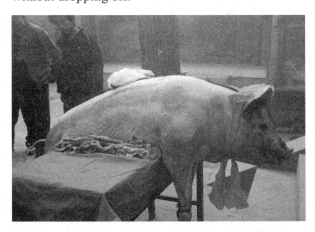

At about three o'clock in the afternoon, the opera troupe of Hebei *bangzi* arrived at Black Dragon Pass while the working crew began to set up the opera stage in an open space beside the temple. According to the arrangement, the troupe would have one performance in the evening and one in the

的人流并不多，除了本乡的，还有一些专门远道而来的香客。香客除了烧香许愿，还围在殿前那块石碑上"粘锅子"，据说如果能把钢锅（硬币）粘在石碑上不掉下来，就能得到龙王爷的庇佑，是个有福之人了。[1]于是香客们怀着许愿的心态，用大拇指用力地把硬币往石碑上按，希望松手那一刻硬币就像用了万能胶一样粘在了石碑上。石碑上的确粘着几十个硬币，长时间都不掉下来。

到了下午三点半左右，乡政府请来的河北梆子剧团到达黑龙关，工作人员开始在庙旁的一大块空地上搭建戏台。按照安排，剧团在当晚和第二天各有一场戏，当晚演的是

---

[1] The custom is a loan from other regions, there was no Dragon God Temple in the past.

---

[1] 这是从外地传入的习俗，过去的龙神庙并不存在。

《窦娥冤》。下午六时，人流渐多，大多数香客手捧的都是高香。六时半，是黄历中一天的吉时，从白云观请来的老道长带领着另外四位道士开始举行第一场祈福法事。老道士穿红底黑纹道袍，戴着一顶配有金色头冠的道士帽。其余四位分别是两男两女，都穿红色道袍，头戴道士帽。道士们手持木鱼、鼓、小钟、磬以及香和供品，先分别向庙内的几个牌位朝拜，然后再

next day, and the repertoire in the evening was *A Sad Story of the Girl Named Dou'e*. At 6:00 p.m., people began to gather around the temple, most of prayers with joss sticks in their hands. At half past six, the so-called lucky time of the day in Chinese almanac, an eminent Taoist priest started the first religious praying ceremony with four fellow priests. The master priest wore a red priest frock with black streaks and a priest hat with a golden crown on it. The fellow priests, two women and two men, all wore red frocks and hats. The priests paid religious homage to several memorial tablets in the temple with a woodblock, a drum, a clock, an inverted bell, incenses and offerings in their hands; then they entered the hall to chant religious scripture for

releasing souls from purgatory. On the altar, dozens of "lucky boxes" were placed in front of the god statue, which were rectangle boxes made of yellow paper; inside each box, there was a piece of cloth on which wrote "presented by follower of God of Dragon" and the name of the follower. During the ceremony, more boxes were placed onto the altar. The first round of religious ceremony lasted for an hour; after a short break for the priests and the bandsmen of the concert, the second round began. This time, besides the priests and bandsmen three prayers came to be enlightened by the scripture. When the right time arrived, the priests put all of the lucky boxes into the censer and burnt them up; it is said that the God of Dragon would bless the followers who have their name on the pieces of cloth inside the boxes.

When night fell, more villagers came to pray and offer the incense from other villages, most of whom would wait till the midnight to worship the gods. The whole evening would be spent in front of the theatre stage where they waited for the performance. At eight o'clock, *A Sad Story of the Girl Named Dou'e* began. In a huge open place, the stage lamp lighted in the dark; the audience in thick cotton-padded coats or down jackets watched

进入正殿内念经超度。这时供桌上已经摆有几十个用以祈福的"吉祥疏袍"供奉在神像前。这些"吉祥疏袍"是一个个用黄纸做成的长方形纸盒，里面都分别装有一表，表上写着"龙神庙×××信士承上"的字样。在法事进行的过程中，还陆续有香客的"吉祥疏袍"呈进殿内。第一场法事大概进行了一个小时，众道士和音乐会的乐手稍息，第二场法事又开始了。这次，殿内除了道士和乐手，还多了三位香客，据说她们是来听经的。等时辰一到，道士就要把经过祈福的"吉祥疏袍"放进香炉中烧掉，据说这是上呈给龙神爷看的，龙神爷看到后就会降福于这些信士。

夜幕降临的时候，从各村前来进香的村民逐渐增多。多数人都要等到子时才上香，所以这时他们都聚在戏台前等着剧团开戏。晚上八时，《窦娥冤》正式拉开帷幕。在一大块空地上，戏台上的大电灯照亮着黑夜，前来看戏的村民穿着厚棉衣或羽绒服，兴致勃勃地站在戏台下看戏。他们最喜欢听的是窦娥的"哭戏"——这次的花旦唱得真不赖。

到了晚上十一时左右（即子时），有些香客从侧门进入庙内，准备上他们的"头炷香"。但更多的香客还是守着午夜十二点的时间，认为那时才是最吉利的时辰。只见，香客们手持高香，按顺序排好队，先来的站在香炉前，后面的人也不往前挤，在香炉前等待着，谁都不愿意提前上香。队伍排成长龙，一直蜿蜒到了庙外。时辰一到，上香的队伍不再齐整，香客从三面围着香炉，争相把香点着，向龙神爷、龙神奶奶拜三拜，然后才放进香炉里。此时，整个龙神庙顿时烟雾缭绕，香火燃烧的火光照得神庙亮如白昼。前来上头炷香的人实在太多，不到3秒钟时间，香炉内已被插满。负责清洁的工作人员不断地从香炉底下铲出香灰，一车一车

the performance in high spirits. The best part of the performance for the villagers was Dou'e's crying out her miserable experience with beautiful and sad songs, as they would comment, "The heroine this year has a wonderful voice."

At around 11 o'clock in the evening, some of the prayers came into the temple from the side gate and waited their turn to burn the first joss stick. Most of the prayers waited until midnight as they believed this was the luckiest moment. The prayers lined up in front of the censer with joss sticks in their hands; the earlier comers stood in the front of the line, and those who stood at the end of the line waited patiently without pushing forward. The line of prayers was winded outside the temple; when midnight fell, the line was no longer in a good order; prayers crowded around the censer, competing with each other to light the joss sticks and kowtowing three times to the God and Goddess of the Dragon before placing them into the censer. The whole dragon temple was soon enveloped in smokes from the incenses and the glow of the burning joss sticks lighted the sky. So many people came for the first joss sticks so that in less than 3 seconds, the censer was filled with joss sticks. Working crew in charge of cleaning the censer spaded out the incense ash from time to time under the bottom of the censer and carried them to the back of the temple.

After burning the joss sticks, the prayers stood in line again to kowtow to the gods and crowded in front of the statutes to pay respect. Prayers came from all age groups, of which the elder prayers took the majority; most of them came from nearby villages, some left their hometown and moved to Liang Town, but every year, when the temple fair is held, they are sure to come to burn the first joss stick. Some of the young people came with their parents to pray for an opportunity to pursue higher education or a promotion in the working place. Some of them believed in the magic power of the gods in the Temple of the God of Dragon since their childhood, so they came with their friends to burn the first joss stick. There were also small children coming with their parents, who sat on father's shoulder and worshipped the god of his or her own Chinese Zodiac; it is said that children who worship

地运到庙后去。

香客烧完香，就要到殿前排队磕头。磕了头，便挤在殿前瞻仰龙神爷龙神奶奶的神像。在庙会进香的香客既有老年人、中年人，也有年轻人。中老年人所占的比重最大，他们大多是附近的村民，也有已经离开本乡，搬到良乡住的，但每年的庙会，他们都会赶过来上头炷香。年轻人中有一些是跟着父母前来，烧香许愿能考上大学，事业能得到提升，也有一些从小就耳濡目染，深信龙神庙的灵验，于是约上同伴一起来挤头炷香。跟着父母来的小孩，此时大都骑在父亲的肩膀上朝拜属于自己的那座生肖神。据说小孩子朝拜生肖神，能得到它的庇佑，从而平安健康，快快长大长高。所以在供奉生肖神的东西配殿内，可以见到不少小孩子磕头朝拜的身影。午夜烧头炷香是每年庙会的高潮，凌晨一点，香客逐渐散去，二月初一的活动也就到此结束了。

their Gods of Chinese Zodiac will be blessed with a healthy life without mishap and grow up strong and tall. Therefore, in the guarding halls on the east and west sides, where the Gods of Chinese Zodiac are enshrined, young children were seen kowtowing and praying. Burning the first joss stick in midnight is the climax of the temple fair; the prayers left for home at one o'clock in the morning and the activities on February 1st came to an end.

三、二月初二：民俗花会汇演

二月初二，经过一晚的喧闹与香火膜拜，黑龙关的天空晴朗无比。这年的二月庙与以往不同的是，乡政府从外地请来了三档比较出名的花会，分别是朝阳区"众友同乐"飞彪吉庆舞狮龙圣会、天桥老艺人宝三的第三代传人"傅氏中幡表演艺术团"，以及丰台"聚义同善"的小车会。为了庙会更加热闹、气派、有序，还邀请了天桥有名的叫卖大王臧鸿担任总主持人。

因为场地有限，本乡的11档花会没有像往年一样，经过土桥子到达庙前

3.Folk Arts Performances on February 2nd

February 2nd saw a clear and sunny day in Black Dragon Pass after the bustling and worshipping night. The February Temple Fairs of this year differed from the previous ones in the folk arts performance, because the township government invited three well-known performing teams: the "Zhong you Tongle (sharing fun with friends)" Lion and Dragon Dancing Group from Chaoyang District, the Flag Dancing Group of Fu Family, who are the third generation of apprentice of the old master artist Baosan from Tianqiao(Bejing Flyover), and the "Juyi Tongshan (sharing goodness)" Trolley Dancing Group from Fengtai District. To make the performance more interesting, the famous host Zang Hong from Tianqiao was invited to host the performance.

Due to the limited space, the eleven performing teams of this town didn't match along the *Tuqiaozi Bridge to perform* in front of the temple such as they did in the previous years, but gave performances in the other side of river opposite to the temple. At eight o'clock in the morning, the eleven performance teams of the local county were gathered on the other bank and lined up from east to west; according to their distance from the Black Dragon Pass, the order was as follows: Fork Performing Team, Waist Drum Dancing and Yangko Dancing from Dongbange Villako, music concert from Shangyingshui Village, Yangko Dancing from Fozizhuang Village, Drum Dancing from Cha'er Village, Yangko Dancing, Trolley Dancing and music concert from Chenjiatai Village, Yangko Dancing from Changcao Village and finally, Yangko Dancing from Black Dragon Pass Village, which was arranged to be the last performer as it was from the host village.

献会，而是安排在庙对岸表演。早晨8时左右，本乡的11档花会已经聚集在龙神庙对岸，按照离黑龙关远近的距离为顺序，从东向西一字排开，分别是：东班各村的叉会，东班各村的腰鼓会，东班各村的秧歌会，上英水村的音乐会，佛子庄村的秧歌会，查儿村的大鼓会，陈家台村的秧歌会，陈家台村的小车会，陈家台村的音乐会，长操村的秧歌会，黑龙关村的秧歌会。黑龙关村属于这一带的主人，安排到最后表演。

此时，前来赶会的群众已经从四面八方陆续来到，龙神庙里挤满了烧香磕头的香客。乡政府在庙旁路边开展了婚育宣传工作，进行"人口与计划生育灯谜有奖竞猜活动"，猜中灯谜立刻领奖，引得许多人驻足竞猜。路对面有几个摆卖供香的小摊，是附近来做生意的村民摆的。

八点半左右，民俗花会汇演正式开始。总主持人臧鸿手持一黄绸旗子主持开幕仪式。在这个仪式上，因为狮子会与中幡会联合献会，所以先要进

this area came to join the temple fair, the Temple of the God of Dragon was crowded with prayers burning the joss sticks and kowtowing. The township government made use of this occasion to promote the policy of population and family plan on the sides of the temple by conducting a lantern riddles contest theme on population and family plan. Those who solved the riddles written on the lanterns were rewarded with gifts immediately, which attracted many passengers to take part in the game. Across the road, there were several stalls to sell the offerings and incenses, the owners of which came from nearby villages.

At about half past eight, the folk arts performances started with the host Zang Hong coming onto the stage with a yellow silk flag. In the opening ceremony, the lion dancing and flag dancing teams would perform together after a meeting ritual, which went as follows, "when the Lion Dancing team

played the music, captains of the two teams greeted three times with the host Zang Hong and each other; for each greeting, the three of them would wave the flag or grasp their hands put in front of their chests(an old Chinese way of greeting) and bow to each other." The ritual was regarded as the meeting of the two teams.

After the meeting ritual, the Flag Dancing Team of Fu Family started their performance first. The members began with a teamwork warming-up: they stood in a line; the first guy threw the flag into the sky and the guy behind him took it and threw it to another guy behind him and it went on; in this way the flag was passed on one by one. It was really an easy job for the performing members. Later they would perform alone one after

another in the following 20 minutes; they performed a series of breathtaking stunts, including the "tooth arrow" and "dragon raises head". The huge flag pole of over 10 meters long with a weight of 40 to 45 kilograms was merely a piece of cake in the hands of the young performers, as they put it on their arms or supported it with their noses, or even supported it with only one finger, which is called "finger

行一个见会仪式。此时，身后狮子会奏乐，两名会首与臧鸿进行"三参"致敬。每"参"一次，他们三人都持旗或抱拳向对方躬身。这样就算是两档花会见过了。

两档花会见过以后，就由傅氏中幡表演艺术团开始献会。幡会成员首先以接龙表演作为热身，他们排成一队，由前一个成员把中幡抛给后面一个成员，一个接一个地抛。这些对幡会成员来说只是小伎俩而已。然后，他们就轮番独自上阵。在20多分钟的献会中，他们先后表演了一系列惊险的高难动作，如"牙箭""龙抬头"等。三丈多高、八九十斤重的中幡在几位年轻的表演者手里好像根本就不算分量。表演者时而将中幡盘在肘上，来个"二郎担山"；时而又用鼻梁托起，表演"断梁"；如此沉重的中幡，表演者还能用五个手指中的任意一指托起，还起了名字叫"串指"；最让老百姓惊呼的绝技是，表演者将用牙托着的中幡高高抛起再用腰接住，之后就地一滚，中幡稳稳落地。这一连串的表演赢得了阵阵掌声。

中幡献会后，狮子会就出场了。两黄两红的四头狮子在臧鸿的引领下先做绕场表演。绕场后，两头黄狮相互配合着做了一系列有难度的动作。它们像是在撒娇一样嬉戏着，分别在地上打滚玩耍。期间，红狮还故意耍到围观

lifting". The most impressive stunt was when the performer supported the flag pole with his teeth and threw it into the air and caught it with his waist, and finally turned over on the ground while the flag pole dropped to the ground stood steadily. The audience all applauded for the wonderful performance.

After the flag performance, it was the turn of Lion Dancing team to perform. Four "lions" (two yellow lions and two red ones) were led by Zang Hong and walked around to greet the audience. The yellow lions then did a series of difficult stunts and rolled on the ground as if playing naughtly, while the red lions danced in front of the audience and made a sudden dive, which scared a little girl to step back. After the red lions' dancing, the yellow

lions climbed up to the four pre-prepared broad tables following the host's Instruction, and the red lions stood by the two sides. Simultaneously, the four lions stood up with four scrolls of writings held in their mouths, reading respectively, "May the favorable weather comes", "Holy land for rain prayers", "May the country be prosperous and people at peace" and "May the land be blessed with a good harvest". Some government officers walked to the lions and took down the scrolls; guests and reporters took this opportunity to take pictures.

Traditionally, the Lion Dancing team is the only team that is allowed to enter the temple. After their performance beside the temple, Zang Hong would lead the four lions to walk along the slope in front of the temple with a yellow flag; the audience followed them to come to an opening outside the temple, which was soon packed with people. The four lions danced again, with crowds of people standing on the ground, on the roofs and on the hills not far away, and all watching the performance joyously. It is believed that only a crowded temple fair can be counted as a success.

A lot of people enjoyed the folk arts performance, while a lot more went to the temple to pray and burn the joss sticks. The long line of prayers was

的群众跟前，一个俯冲，让小女孩吓得往后退了一大步。在红狮表演之后，黄狮在臧鸿的指令下，登上事先准备好的四个大板桌，两头红狮也各自走到黄狮两旁。一声令下，四头狮子分别叼着四幅写着"风调雨顺""祈雨圣地""国泰民安""五谷丰登"的春联站立起来。这时，乡政府干部走向狮子，取下这四幅春联。众多应邀前来的贵宾、记者都不失时机地起立拍照。

按照传统，狮子会是唯一可以进入庙里的花会。在庙旁献会后，臧鸿手持黄绸旗，引领四头狮子沿着庙前斜坡来到庙前的空地上，围观群众跟随前行，小小空地被围得水泄不通。四头狮子再次耍闹起来，人群拥挤，不但平地上站满了人，连屋顶上、山上也站满了。按照当地观念，庙会要的就是这份挤，这才算喜庆、热闹。

看花会表演的人多，庙里虔诚上香的香客更多。进香的队伍一直维持着良好的秩序，排队上香磕头，在心里默念着自己的愿望。香客多是附近的乡民，平时相熟却不多见面，烧完香便聚在一起唠嗑。当狮子会从正门进来时，大家都不约而同地鼓掌。这年的狮子会与往常一样，由正门进来"参龙神"。臧鸿在前，四头狮子摇头摆尾陆续走进庙里，一字排开。臧鸿以他洪亮的嗓音说道："3月9日，农历二月二，我们金盏乡狮子老会朝拜龙

in a good order; when it was their turn, they would burn the joss sticks, kowtow to the gods and say silently about their wishes in the heart. Most of the prayers coming on this day were from the nearby villages; they were acquainted with each other but seldom met; they would get together after the praying ceremony and chat for a while. When the lions danced into the front gate, the audience all rose and applauded. The lion dancing of this year came to greet the God of Dragon as the previous years. Following Zang Hong, the four lions walked into the temple shaking their heads and waving their tails, and lined up in front of the statues of gods. Zang Hong said in his loud and clear voice, "The day of March 9th is February 2nd of Chinese

lunar calendar, the Lion Dancing team from Jinzhan Town is coming to pay respect to the Temple of the God of Dragon, three kowtows to the God of Dragon, three kowtows! " Then, he knelt down and began to kowtow, followed by the head of the lion dancing team and the four lions; the music was on and they gave the God and Goddess of Dragon three kowtows. After that, the four lions clapped their "claws" to the God of Dragon to show respect. After the performance in the temple, the lion dancing team, with groups of people clustering around, returned to the opening in front of the temple for another round of performance.

After that, the Trolley Dancing Team and the theatre troupe of Hebei *bangzi* were ready to perform. The repertoire played was *Ascend the Throne*. The Trolley Dancing Team was also called Cloud Trolley Team or Happy Trolley Team, their performing tools were mainly the trolleys. This time "Juyi Tongshan (sharing goodness)" Trolley Dancing Group invited had a large crew with over 20 actors and actresses, they were: the Lady sitting on the trolley (wearing heavy make-up and gorgeously dressed), the girl who pulled the trolley (with plait, dressed in colored clothes), the maids walking aside the trolley (two farmer girls), the old man who pushed the trolley (with beard), the Handsome Fan (a handsome young man with a paper fan in hand), the ugly Fan (a clown-look young man with a paper fan in hand), the ugly old woman (with a big tobacco bag in hand), the blind man (wearing a pair of dark glasses, holding

神庙，向龙神叩拜！三参叩拜！"说完，他跪下叩头，狮子会会首带领着四头狮子在奏乐的配合下，向着龙神爷、龙神奶奶致了"三参叩拜"。"三参"后，四头狮子在原地"打掌"，意思是狮子向龙神叩首，以示虔诚。在庙里献艺后，狮子会就在群众的簇拥下从侧门再次来到庙前空地表演。

随后，守候在庙旁空地的小车会和河北梆子剧团分别开始表演。河北梆子剧团唱的是《大登殿》。小车会又叫"云车会"或"太平车"，其主要表演道具是小车。这次请来的"聚义同善小车会"阵容庞大，角色就有20多个，主要有：坐车的娘娘（浓施粉黛，花枝招展），拉车的姑娘（留辫子，身穿彩衣彩裤），扶车的丫环（为2人，佃子打扮），推车的老汉（带胡子），文扇（俊扮公子，手持纸扇），武扇（丑扮公子，手持纸扇），丑老妪（即丑婆子，手持大烟袋），盲人（戴黑边眼镜，手拿马杆），和尚（身穿破僧衣，头顶济公帽，脖挂长念珠，手持破扇），傻柱子（头梳冲天绺小辫），傻丫头（头梳刷子小辫）。他们以锣鼓唢呐等乐器伴奏，表演的动作比较接近生活。群众们围着小车会看得不亦乐乎：丑婆耍烟袋、转手帕、卧鱼叼花，和尚表演转佛珠、反扑、过桥等武生动作，盲人丢马杆、摔跤、过河等。许多老百姓嫌在平地上看不清楚，干

a blind stick), a monk (wearing a torn frock and a monk cap with the prayers' beads hung around the neck and a torn fan in hand), the boy (a pigtail on head pointing up) and the girl (two brush-like pigtails pointing up). They marched along with music played by gongs, drums and suona horns; their performances were lively and funny, which made the audience around them laugh again and again. The ugly old woman would play stunts with her tobacco bag and her handkerchief, the monk performed a series of martial actions, such as rotating the necklace, turning a somersault and crossing the bridge (a kind of moves of martial role in Chinese Opera); the blind man threw the stick, pretended to tumble and looked for his way of crossing the "river". Some of the audience even

climbed up along the hill nearby to get a clearer view of the performance.

After the performance by the three teams, the villagers went along the levee to the other bank, waiting for the performances of the eleven teams from their own villages. According to the arrangement, the village teams stood at the place where they lined up previously and began their performances in order, starting from the east to the west. Due to the time limits, the authorities set the performing time for every team with the longest performance of ten minutes. The performances were splendid as every village showed their own features, which won bursts of applause from the audience. At noon, the Folk Arts Performance came to an end, and thus people reluctantly left the Temple of the God of Dragon.

脆爬到山坡上，以俯视的角度把小车会的表演看个一清二楚。

村民在庙前看完三档花会表演，心里记挂着本村来的花会，于是便陆续从大堤走到对岸，等待本乡的11档花会献会。在统一指挥下，潭对岸的本乡花会以从东向西的顺序在原地开始献会。这次花会汇演因为时间关系，乡政府给每个花会限定了表演时间，最长的献会表演也不超过10分钟。各村的花会都有各自的特色，演出十分精彩，不时博得阵阵掌声。到了中午时分，这次"民俗花会汇演"正式降下帷幕，人们恋恋不舍地陆续离开龙神庙。

冀南"龙牌会"
Dragon Tablet Club in the South of Hebei

河北赵县，位于石家庄市东部，即历史上有名的赵州，境内有闻名中外的赵州桥（安济桥）和佛名远播的柏林寺。范庄是赵县的一个乡镇，因每年举办二月二龙牌会而名声在外，吸引大批学者和游客前来参加。龙牌会是范庄人一年一度的节日。在村民的观念中，正月十五不算是个隆重的节日，他们认为只有过了二月二，年才算结束。范庄龙牌会庙会会期是从二月初一到初四，在庙会期间，有盛大的"游龙牌"、念佛、秧歌表演、放焰火、看戏等多种活动，热闹非常。

Zhao County of Hebei Province is on the east of Shijiazhuang and was the famous Zhaozhou in history, where stands the world-famous Zhaozhou Bridge (Anji Bridge) and the well-known Bailin Temple. Fanzhuang is a small town within the county; it is known for its annual Dragon Tablet Club, which attracts a large number of scholars and visitors every year. Dragon Tablet Club becomes an annual festival for local villagers, to whom only February 2nd marks the end of Spring Festival, not the Lantern Festival on January 15th. The Temple Fair of Dragon Tablet Club in Fanzhuang starts from February 1st to 4th, during which there are various activities, such as the grand "Dragon Tablet Marching", Buddha praying, Yangko performing, firework display and theatres.

1. The history of Dragon Tablet Club

There is a legend about the origin of Dragon Tablet Club. The older generation believes that the Dragon Tablet is worshipped in memory of Goulong, who was born on February 2nd. Who is this man that people all respect and admire? It is said that in the in the ancient times ancient times, since Pangu separated the earth from the heaven and created everything on it, mankind started to live together in tribes; the head of the tribes was Gonggongshi, who was said to be a powerful hero with a human face and a body of serpent and led the tribes to make a living by hunting. Later a man named Zhuanxu had a quarrel with Gonggongshi over the territory, which led to a fierce fighting between them. The fight made the sky murky and the earth dark with sands and stones sweeping along the ground. The fight left a huge hole in the sky and the rain began to fall without stopping; soon the flood inundated the earth and threatened the lives of all living creatures. It was Nuwa the Goddess who made every effort to collect enough peddles and stones to patch the sky. As Gonggongshi was defeated, his son Goulong was also driven away from their old territory, so he led the tribes to Fanzhuang to make a fresh start and rebuild their home. At that time, there were flood everywhere; fortunately, Goulong was a great hero with the power of toppling the mountains and overturning the seas, so he regulated the rivers and brought back the farmlands with the help of his fellow tribesmen. After that, people survived on

一、龙牌会的历史

关于龙牌会的来历，当地有一个传说：老一辈人说龙牌是纪念勾龙的，勾龙是二月二生日，这里的老百姓十分崇拜勾龙。勾龙是谁呢？相传遥远的古代，自盘古氏开天辟地造出万物，人类就有了部落，部落首领叫共工氏。传说共工氏是一个人面蛇身、能耐很大的人物，他带领部落以打猎为主。后来，一个叫颛顼的，与共工氏争地盘，二人大战起来，只战得天昏地暗、飞沙走石，以至于把天打了个窟窿，从此大雨下个不止，沥水成灾，万物难以生存，害得女娲氏花了很大工夫炼石才把天补好。共工氏被战败，共工氏的儿子勾龙也被赶得无法存身。最后，勾龙带部落来到范庄一带另辟天地。那时候遍地都是洪水，无法打猎，勾龙有排山倒海的本领，便带领部落治水造田，栽培谷物。从那时起，人们以食五谷生存下来。勾龙带着部落过着安居乐业的生活。可是颛顼时有侵吞之心，一次将勾龙部落围困得风雨不透。颛顼要勾龙让出领导地位。勾龙为了拯救部落，便化为一道白气，变成一只白蛾，飘然而去。每年正月一过，范庄一带便常有白蛾翩翩飞来，人们便认为是勾龙显圣。为表示对勾龙的崇敬，人们设龙牌来供奉，龙牌就是勾龙的化身。

1927年出生的罗庆祥是龙牌会的老会头，在他的眼中康熙年间范庄就有了龙牌会。那时龙牌会规模小，二月二上供，但究竟起源于何时已不知道了。范庄及附近的任庄、曹庄都是沙河（应是滹沱河）的故道。沙河改道后，这一带全是沙土，天特别干旱，人们只能靠天吃饭，经常是五、六月还没有安上苗，地里光秃秃的，生活特别困难。这样过了几年，就有几位老人在二月二出来，搬几张桌子搭个庙，摆个神位供奉起来，看能否下雨。供龙

the five cereals they grew and lived and worked in peace and contentment. However, the aggressive and greedy Zhuanxu once again surrounded Goulong's tribes and demanded that Goulong gave up his leadership. To save the people of tribes from another war, surrounded by invisible gas, Goulong turned into a white moth and left his beloved tribes. Every year when January ends, there were always white moths flying near Fanzhuang, which people believe is the apparition of Goulong. To show their respect to the hero, they enshrine the Dragon Tablet, which they worship as the incarnation of Goulong.

According to Luo Qingxiang, the head of the Dragon Tablet Club who was born in 1927, the Club was there in Fanzhuang ever since the Reign of Emperor Kangxi. At that time, the size of the Club was small and they worshipped the tablet on the Day of February 2nd, and no one knew when the club began. Fanzhuang and the nearby Renzhuang and Caozhuang were previously the waterways of Sha River; after the river changed its route, the three areas were often covered with sand and became too dry to grow any crops. People made a difficult living at the mercy of the heaven when there were no crops in the bare field in May and June. Finally, several years later, some old men set up a temple with a few tables on February 2nd so that they could enshrine a tablet for gods to pray for rainfall. The Dragon Tablet was made for the Dragon God who was in charge of the rain. People promised to the Dragon God that if he brought the rainfall within seven days, they would worship him generation by generation. As a result, four or five days later, the rain came and the crops were planted in the field. Villagers were so happy that they bought vegetables and made pancakes in partnership to offer to the Tablet and worshipped the God of Dragon, the practice of which was passed down by generations.

2. The Dragon Ancestor Hall

Dragon Ancestor Hall of Fanzhuang was built on February 2nd of the lunar calendar in 2003, which was also the Dragon Culture Museum of Zhaozhou. As you are approaching the Dragon Ancestor Hall, the first thing to come into your eyes is a yellow scroll of painting with nine dragons on it; below there is a red scroll and the inscription on it reads "all Chinese descendants are the sons and daughters of the Dragon". There are also writings on the four pillars in front of the Dragon Ancestor Hall, such as "old custom, ancient practice and time-honored tradition relive in an antique town", "the charm of dragon, the love for dragon and the culture of dragon are worshipped by dragon's descendants", "the hearts of dragon's descendants are closely linked", etc. On the two sides of the gate of the Dragon Ancestor Hall are two plates put up, the one on the left reads "Dragon Culture Museum of Zhaozhou, China", the one on the right reads "Dragon Tablet Club of Fanzhuang in Zhao County, Hebei Province".

需龙牌，就做了龙牌——龙的牌位，求雨。一开始向龙牌许愿：七天内下了雨就世代供奉。结果，四五天时就下了雨，庄稼种上了。大家很高兴，便开始合伙买菜、做大馍供奉龙牌，并一代一代地传下来了。

二、走进龙祖殿

范庄的龙祖殿在2003年农历二月二日落成，它同时还是赵州龙文化博物馆。走进龙祖殿，首先看到的是画了九条龙的黄色横幅。这条横幅往里偏下是一条写着"炎黄子孙都是龙的传人"的红色横幅。龙祖殿前面的四根柱子上分别写着"古镇设醮，古风古俗古传统；传人祭祖，龙情龙韵龙文化""龙的传人永远心连心"等。龙祖殿门口左右分别挂两块牌子，左边是"中国赵州龙文化博物馆"，右边是"河北省赵县范庄龙牌会"。

进入大殿，第一眼看到的是很气派的木刻龙牌，它身上披着霞帔（霞帔外边是红绸，里边是黄绸），被摆放在龙祖殿最显耀的位置。左右分别置有两把很气派的龙椅，龙椅上雕刻着龙的图案，上面放了黄色的垫子。椅子后边是两个充满了传统气息的大花瓷瓶，花瓶里插满了塑料荷花。龙牌左边置有华盖，华盖由深红、紫红、黄色绸缎制成，上面绣有龙的图案。另外，龙牌左右还分置两把扇，

When entering the Dragon Ancestor Hall, the first thing you see is a glorious Dragon Tablet carved in wood and half-covered with a colorful cape (red silk outside and yellow silk inside), which is placed in the most eye-catching position in the hall. On the left and right of the Tablet, there are two big chairs with images of dragons carved on them and each has a yellow cushion. Behind the chairs, there are two tall and antique china vases painted with flowers and plastic lotus flowers are put in each of them. On the left side of the Tablet, there is an imperial canopy made of silk in dark red, purple and yellow with embroidered dragons on it. Besides, the Tablet is accompanied by two fans on each side with patterns of dragons and phoenixes on them. On the altar where the Tablet is placed, there are two small vases on each side with lotus in them, too; in front of the Tablet are things offered for sacrifice, including fruits such as apples, bananas, oranges, pitayas and coconuts, and five flowers made of flour. The number of each offerings is often in odd numbers such as three or five, instead of even numbers such as four or six.

扇面为黄色，上面贴有龙和凤的图案。在摆放龙牌的供桌上，其左右分别放了两个小花瓶，花瓶里插的也是荷花，其前方摆满了供品，包括各种水果，如苹果、香蕉、橙子、火龙果、椰子等，还有五个面花。所有供品数量一般为三、五等单数，避免四、六等双数。

Two graceful lotus lights are placed beside the Tablet, one on each side. On the right there is a locked red wooden box, on the top of which are bundles of joss sticks and an earthen bowl. Inside the box are incomes of the Dragon Tablet Club, and in front of the box is a paper-made shallow

龙牌前方的左右两边还摆放了两个造型优美的荷花电灯。龙牌右前方放有一个上了锁的红木箱即功德箱，上面放了几把香和一个钵。红木箱里盛放的是龙牌会期间的功德钱，红木箱前边有一个纸笸箩。这个笸箩也是用来盛放香客们捐赠香火钱的。龙牌左前方放的是一个玻璃盒子，里边盛着几只白蛾。这些白蛾是龙牌爷的化身。当有香客来的时候，龙牌前边的香炉和白蛾前边的香炉可同时烧香，负责看香的人也可以同时给多个香客看香。供复前面放了三个红色的垫子，供来烧香的香客磕头使用。供复两边，分别有两把铺了红布的长椅，供香客坐着休息。庙会期间，龙牌前的香火一直不断，从四面八方赶来的香客在龙牌前磕头、打香、问吉凶。所以，桌子下边还放了两个盛着水的盆，以便随时将燃烧着的香淹灭。

龙牌的后面，与龙牌背对的是观音像，与观音正对的是圣人、佛祖、老君像。龙牌会曾经用过的四块小型的龙牌被摆放在大殿西北角墙根。这四个小型龙牌，最大的高度也不过一米多一点，最小的

basket, where prayers place their lucky money. On the left there is a box made of glass, inside of which lie several white moths as a symbol of Goulong, the Dragon Tablet God. When prayers come, the censers in front of the Dragon Tablet and of the white moths can burn joss sticks at the same time, and the man in charge of the burnt incenses can serve more than one prayers at the same time. On the ground of the Dragon Tablet, three red cushions are placed for prayers to kneel on when kowtowing. There are also two benches covered with red cloth for prayers to sit on and rest. During the temple fairs, the incenses of Dragon Tablet never go out, as prayers come in endless streams from far and near to kowtow in front of the Dragon Tablet, burn the incenses and divine. Under the table, there are two basins of water to put out the burning incenses at any time.

Behind the Dragon Tablet, standing against it on the back, is the statue of Buddhist god Guanyin; facing to Guanyin are statues of Confucius, the Buddha and Most Exalted Lord Lao. Four smaller Dragon Tablets used to be worshipped by the Club are placed at the northwest corner of the hall, the tallest of which is less than over one meter, and the smallest is half the size of the middle one. The main bodies of the four Dragon Tablets are made of thin metal boards except that the bases of them are woodenly made with images of dragons carved on.

Behind the Dragon Ancestor Hall is a shed set up, inside of which hang about 150 holy cards. On the two sides outside the Dragon Ancestor Hall, two water vats are placed with some water and a stick in each of them. When prayers passed by, they would stir the stick in the vat three times clockwise and three times anticlockwise while chanting, "Stir the vat to stay away from the sore; stir the urn to stay away from illness."

3.Rituals of Dragon Tablet Club

The ceremony of Dragon Tablet Club lasts four days, from February 1st to February 4th, during which members of Club greet and see off the God of Dragon Tablet and other gods according to certain rituals.

则只有这中间最大的那一个的一半大小。这四个龙牌主体部分全部是用薄板制成，底座也是木制的，上面画有龙的图案。

在龙祖殿后面搭有一处醮棚，里面悬挂了众多神码，总数在150幅左右。在龙祖殿的两边，还分别放了两个水缸，水缸里盛了一些水，放了一根棍，香客们路过的时候，用棍子在缸里左转三圈，右转三圈，边转边说："捣捣缸，不生疮；捣捣瓮，不生病。"

三、龙牌会的仪式过程

龙牌会的会期总共有四天，从二月初一开始，到二月初四结束。在这四天中，龙牌会里的人会按照一定的程序迎接龙牌爷以及其他众神的到来，并在庙会结束之时送走他们。

龙牌会过会的程序

日期	活动
二月初一	戒五荤、游龙牌①、花会表演、念佛、看香
二月初二	念佛、花会表演、看香、响棚②、上大供、放焰火
二月初三	念佛、看香
二月初四	念佛、看香、发大纸、落棚③、舍饭、出水

Rituals of Dragon Tablet Club

Date	Activity
Feb. 1st	stop eating meats, Dragon Tablet Marching①, folk arts performances, worshipping the Buddha, burning the incenses
Feb. 2nd	worshipping the Buddha, folk arts performances, burning the incenses, setting off firecrackers②, offering sacrifices, firework performance
Feb. 3rd	worshipping the Buddha, burning the incenses
Feb. 4th	worshipping the Buddha, burning the incenses, burning lucky papers, pulling down the shed③, offering porridge, offering meals to spirits

（一）游龙牌

二月初一之前，范庄人就搭好醮棚，将神码按顺序挂好。二月初一早上，周边村落的花会、秧歌队陆续来到龙祖殿，先在龙祖殿里磕个头，然后表演。这时，龙牌会里的人在龙祖殿前烧了一堆香纸，叫作发大醮。十几

a.Dragon Tablet Marching

Before February 1st, people from Fanzhuang set up the shed and put up the holy cards in order. On the morning of February 1st, folk arts teams and Yangko performers come to the Dragon Ancestor Hall and kowtow to the gods before their performances. At that time, some members of the

---

①二月初一主要是游龙牌的活动。在龙祖殿落成之前，龙牌会经历了从上一轮值会头家到下一轮值会头家的过程，龙牌安置地点的迁移就是不可避免的，因此有了盛大的游龙牌的活动。龙祖殿落成之后，理论上游龙牌活动变成并不是非举行不可的仪式了，但由于其他各种原因，游龙牌活动在经历了短暂的取消之后，重新又出现在龙牌会上。除了游龙牌活动之外，烧香、念佛的队伍也在这一天就赶到范庄，加上蜂拥而至的香客，龙祖殿殿里殿外一片热闹。
②响棚是以放鞭炮的形式请全神的仪式，放过鞭炮之后就标志着所有的神仙都被请来了。
③落棚是指拆除醮棚。

---

①It is the main activity on February 1st. Dragon Tablet Club was passed on from one family to another before the Dragon Ancestor Hall was built. Thus the Tablet was always moved to different places, and the practice of Dragon Tablet Marching is established in this way. Though the ritual is not necessary now as the Dragon Ancestor Hall is built, for some reasons, the Marching is maintained after a short calling-off, and reappears in the Club activities. Besides the Marching, large numbers of prayers also swarm to the Fanzhuang and the Hall is burst with noise and excitement.
②Setting off the firecrackers is a way to invite all of the gods; it is believed that all of the gods would come after the firecrackers.
③It refers to pulling down the place for religious ritual.

Dragon Tablet Club would burn a pile of incense papers when dozens of women chant ballads to invite the God of Dragon. At about nine o'clock, the grand Dragon Tablet Marching begins. Eight or nine strong men carry the Dragon Tablet from the Dragon Ancestor Hall into the opening in front of it and lay the Tablet steadily on the ground. The colorful cape covering the Tablet is reset, which is red outside and yellow inside, before the marching starts. In the front of the marching crowd several young men fire with blunderbusses from time to time and a young man following them lifts a flag of command. The Dragon Tablet is placed in a big sedan of yellow curtains, surrounded by eight triangle-shaped yellow flags fluttering in the wind. There are also some paper-flower-made decorations in various colors held by villagers of Fanzhuang in the marching crowds. Some women walk in the flag team as they are the team of Dragon Basket, which is a wooden stick of one-and-half meters long representing the yellow dragon, with two baskets

个妇女念诵"请龙经"，请龙神降临。九时许，盛大的"游龙牌"仪式正式开始。八九个壮劳力从龙祖殿里把龙牌抬到龙祖殿前的空地上，放稳。人们先整理龙牌所披的霞帔。霞帔由两件套组成的，外边是红色的，里边是金色的。整理好之后，游龙的队伍出发。在队伍的最前面是几个青年男子，他们不定时地放土铳，一个青年男子举着令旗紧随其后。再往后就是龙牌坐落其中的黄幔大轿，轿子周边是八面三角形的大黄旗迎风招展，一些花花绿绿的纸花扎成的物品也由范庄人擎着前行。和旗幡队伍混在一起的是由几个妇女组成的挑经担的队伍，范庄龙牌会的经担是龙担。龙担的主体是一米半左右长度的黄龙的造型，下边挑两个装满花束的花篮。两个妇女挑着龙担，其他一些妇女扭着秧歌前行。在龙轿前行的过程中，有一些妇女始终面对龙牌，双手合十，倒退行走。这样做的目的除了表示对龙神爷的敬重之外，还有注意龙牌前的安全的意思。走到一些地方，游龙的队伍会稍微停一下。例如，当游龙的队伍快要转到范庄村委会的时候，在水泥路上，队伍停了一下。当队伍停下来的时候，双手合十、倒退行走的妇女便跪下来。来自周边村落的花会表演队跟在后面，一路吹吹打打，很是热闹。

浩浩荡荡的游龙队伍极大地吸引了村民们的目光。早在游龙牌活动开始之前，许多村民就已经从家里出来，翘首等在游龙牌要经过的地方。一些父母抱着孩子站在街头，一些老太太还特意搬把椅子坐到街头看热闹，整个场面热闹非常。同时，也有一些虔诚的人会在龙牌经过的时候，跪着迎接龙牌的到来。

filled with bouquets and tied to the two ends of it. Two of the women carry the baskets while the rest of the team proceed in Yangko dance. As the Dragon sedan moves forward, some women in front of the sedan would turn backward to face Dragon Tablet while still walking, with their palms put together. This is not only a way to show respect to the God of Dragon Tablet, but also to remind the sedan carriers to be careful about the road condition in front of the sedan. The marching crowds will take a rest when they have walked a certain distance. For example, when they are near the village committee building of Fanzhuang, they will stop on the cement road, while the backward-walking women kneel down. Folk arts performing teams from neighboring villages follow the marching crowds while blowing the trumpets and striking the drums, which is a very lively and exciting scene.

The large crowds of Dragon Tablet Marching attract a lot of villagers, who leave their home long before the marching starts, and wait impatiently along the marching route. In this joyous moment, there are parents standing on the street with babies in their arms and some old women even take a chair with them to sit on while waiting. Some pious prayers would kneel down when the sedan passes by to greet the Dragon Tablet.

At around eleven o'clock, the marching crowds return to the Dragon Ancestor Hall, and the Dragon Tablet is placed in the Dragon Ancestor Hall again. Women in the Club would do the cleaning work in front of the Tablet, as prayers from all over the area come to kneel down in front of the Tablet and pray for the blessings from the God of Dragon Tablet. Members of the Club are busy burning the incenses for the prayers and keeping the orders inside and outside the Dragon Ancestor Hall.

b.Offering Sacrifice

It is an important activity to offer sacrifice to all of the gods and spirits, which means that all of them are invited to the celebration. Generally speaking, after setting off the firecrackers on the afternoon of February 2nd, it is time to offer sacrifice in front of

十一点左右，游龙的队伍回到龙祖殿，龙牌被重新安置在龙祖殿里。会里的妇女将龙牌前面收拾好，四面八方拥来的香客跪到龙牌前求龙牌爷保佑，帮会的人们开始忙着为香客们看香并维持各处的安全。

（二）上大供

给所有神灵上供是庙会期间的一项重要活动。这项活动标志着节日期间所有的神灵都被请到了。一般而言，初二下午响棚

之后，就要上大供，包括在龙牌前摆五个面花、五碗素菜、五碗清水，另外在其他主要神灵面前也至少放一碗素菜、一碗清水。放好之后，一些妇女分成几组在神灵面前焚香、烧纸、磕头，在烧过纸之后，一人喊"南无"，其他人和"阿弥陀佛"，这是隆重地请神吃饭的意思。据女会首米秋改说，一般初二下午供上，初三早上三点左右撤供，这就表示初二和初三都供上了。

（三）放焰火

初二晚上，是传统的放焰火活动。从晚上7点半左右，范庄就热闹起来。许多人吃晚饭后即拥向龙祖殿。一些年轻的父母抱着孩子或者是将孩子驮在肩膀上去看焰火。总体来看，喜欢看放焰火的以年轻的村民为主。在放焰火活动开始之前，人们也在龙祖殿以及龙祖殿后面的醮棚里转两圈，磕个头烧炷香。在这个时候，一些商贩也赶来卖形态各异的荧光棒，也有一些

the Dragon Tablet, including five crispy dumplings, five vegetable dishes, and five bowls of clear water. In addition, at least one vegetable dish and one bowl of rinsing should be placed in front of the other gods and spirits. After that, a few women are divided into several groups to burn the incenses and lucky papers and kowtow to the gods. When the papers are burnt, one of them chants "Namo", and others follow her by chanting "Amitabha", which means to invite the gods to a grand dinner. According to Mi Qiugai who is the chief of these women, the offerings are often placed on the afternoon of February 2nd, and put away at three o'clock in the morning on February 3rd, which means that there are offerings on both of the two days.

c.Firework Performance

The evening of February 2nd is the time for traditional firework performance. From about half past seven in the evening, the Fanzhuang is bathed in a joyous atmosphere when crowds of people come to the Dragon Ancestor Hall after dinner. Some young parents carry the children in their arms or on the shoulder to see the fireworks. Generally speaking, the audience of firework performance is mainly made of younger villagers. Before the fireworks begin, people will walk around the Dragon Ancestor Hall and the shed behind the Hall, kowtowing and burning the incenses. Some peddlers come to sell light sticks which give out colorful lights and other retailers sell snacks in their trolleys. The Dragon Ancestor Hall stands out from the dark night in the lights from the sticks of children's hands and the opening in front of the Dragon Ancestor Hall becomes noisier. Before the performance begins at eight o'clock, there are already some fireworks in the sky above Fanzhuang. When the performing time arrives, the sky is lit by all kinds of fireworks everywhere, and in front of the Dragon Ancestor Hall, huge crowds of people leave no more space for new comers. As beautiful flowers of fireworks blossom in the sky, the crowds on the ground give out exciting shouts and the festival atmosphere rises again in the night sky.

d. Burning Lucky Papers, Offering Porridge and Offering Meals to Spirits

Activities on the third day are much less than in the second day of February, and on the fourth day, there is no activity at all, as it is the day to see off the gods. Before the gods leave, the Club starts the ceremony of "burning lucky paper", which is hosted by a woman. During the ceremony, people burn incenses, papers, paper-made gold and silver ingots. A group of women chant the Buddha scriptures while burning the paper.

Besides, there are also the rituals of "offering porridge" and "offering meals to spirits". Porridge offering begins on the fourth day of February; it is

人在小推车上卖小吃。许多小孩子手里拿着在夜空中如霓虹般闪烁的荧光棒摇来摇去，龙祖殿前更显热闹了。放焰火的活动在8点左右开始，但在这之前，就有零星的焰火开始点亮范庄的夜空。快到8点的时候，焰火开始布满龙祖殿前的天空，范庄龙祖殿前已经是人山人海，找个立足之地都困难了。各种各样多彩的图案在天空中绽放，人群中不时传来尖叫声，节日的气氛在夜空中再次浓郁起来。

（四）发大纸、舍饭和出水

初三的活动较之初二就少了，初四庙会上基本无事，这一天要送神离开。送神之前，会里的人们要举行"发大纸"的仪式。这个仪式也由女性主持。发大纸的时候，人们烧很多香、纸、金银元宝之类的。发大纸的时候也要念佛，一群妇女边烧边念佛经。

除此之外还有"舍饭"和"出水"两个仪式活动。舍饭是在初四当天向众人施舍小米粥的活动，这是老一辈传下来的，当地人认为这样的饭吃了好。"出水"是打发孤魂野鬼的仪式。出水的时候，会上要准备很多元宝和8桶饭，这些饭包括米、面、馍馍、饼干、菜之类的，拉着到梨园里去。在四个路口，每个路口舍两桶饭。据说，在举行"出水"仪式的时候，"留在龙牌的人们需要一直跪着，直到去'出水'的人们回来，鸣炮以示结束"①。

（五）念佛

庙会期间，来龙牌会上念佛的群体很多。一般而言，这些念佛的队伍由十几个人组成，念佛的以中老年女性为主，在念佛的队伍里配乐的又以老年男性为主。服饰上，多为平常打扮，以素色衣服为主。外村念佛的来到龙牌会上，一

①盛燕、赵旭东：《从"家"到"庙"——一个华北乡村庙会的仪式变迁》，黄宗智主编《中国乡村研究》.第六辑，福州：福建教育出版社，2008年，第117页。

a practice for generations as people believe that it brings luck and fortune to those who eat the porridge on that day. "Offering meals to spirits" is a ritual to send off the spirits and ghosts. The Club will prepare some gold and silver ingots and eight barrels of food, including rice, noodles, steamed buns, biscuits and vegetables, which are carried to the theater. There are four crossroads on the way, and two of the eight barrels are placed at each crossroad. It is said that when the ceremony is going on, those who stay with the Dragon Tablet should kneel down on the ground until people come back from the food offering ceremony and the whole ritual ends with firecrackers.[1]

e. Worshipping the Buddha

A large number of people come to the Dragon Tablet Club to worship the Buddha during the

[1] Sheng Yan, Zhao Xudong, *From "Home" To "Temple": the Change of Rituals of The Temple Fair in the Countryside Of North China*, Edited by Huang Zongzhi, *Studies On the Countryside Of China*, Volume 6, Fujian Education Publishing House, 2008, p.117.

temple fair period. Generally speaking, prayers are composed of mainly women of middle and old age, there being dozens of them; and the music players among the prayers are mostly old men. People attending the worshipping ceremony are all dressed in their usual plain clothes. Prayers from other villages would worship the Dragon Tablet first and then the other gods. Musical instruments included in the ceremony are Dang (a folk musical instrument), earth bowl, cymbals and drums. *Dang* is called *"Dangdangge"* by local people, which is a piece of bowl-sized round copper fixed on two wooden sticks. The two sticks are tied as a cross, the thwartwise one is shorter while the vertical one is longer. The more refined *Dang* has some decorative patterns and shapes on the surface of the copper. The *Dangs* in Dragon Tablet Club are all carved with images of dragon and decorated with colorful cloth. A variety of Buddha songs are chanted and played on temple fairs. Whenever a passage of scriptures is finished, prayers all kneel down and the leading prayer calls "Namo" while others follow by chanting "Amitabha". Most of the women prayers believe in the gods and wish to be blessed with a happy life without mishap by worshipping and chanting in front of the gods.

f.Folk Arts Performances

Folk Arts Performance is an integrate part of Dragon Tablet Club ceremony. When the temple fair begins, performing teams from neighboring villages come to Fanzhuang and make their joyous poses on the stage, which attract crowds of

般先要在龙祖殿前对着龙牌念，念完之后再给其他神仙念。念佛所用的乐器包括铛、钵、镲、鼓等，"铛"在当地被称为"当当格"（音），简单的是由两块木棍固定一个碗口大小的铜面。横着的木棍要短一些，竖着的木棍要长一些，复杂一点的还在固定这个铜面的小木棍上雕刻一些花纹和形状，范庄龙牌会里的当当格一般都雕刻有龙的形状，当当格的最上面扎一些颜色鲜丽的布。庙会上所念的佛歌种类众多。每当一段经歌念完的时候，所有人都会跪下，领头的人喊"南无"，其他人喊"阿弥陀佛"。大部分参与念佛的妇女都笃信众神，相信通过在神灵面前念佛会换得平安。

（六）花会表演

花会表演也是龙牌会的重要组成部分。每到庙会的时候，周围村落的表演队伍来到范庄在龙祖殿前热热闹闹地舞动起来，

吸引了众多的目光。这些花会表演有传统的秧歌表演，有军乐表演，也有震天的锣鼓队伍，还有少量自编自演的现代舞。花会表演队伍的着装一般很亮眼，基本上每一队都统一着装，服装大都选红、绿、黄等鲜亮的颜色。

（七）看香

看香是庙会上的一项重要内容，当地人更经常称其为"打香"。每到庙会时节，香客们从四面八方拥向龙牌会，在龙牌会上的诸神仙面前为自己或是家人烧香。如果要请

villagers. The performances vary from traditional Yangko Dancing, military music parade and gong and drum playing, to the modern dance. The performers are dressed in an eye-catching way as most of the team uniforms are in bright color such as red, green and yellow.

g.Burning the Incense

Burning the incense is another important event on temple fair, which is called by the local people as "striking the incense". When it's time for the temple fair, prayers from all over the area take part in the Dragon Tablet Club ceremony and burn the incenses for their family members or themselves in front of the statues of gods. Prayers ask for a future divination from a Club member by saying, "Please strike the incenses for me." In general, prayers all bring joss sticks, gold and silver ingots, torch papers and cookies to the temple fair; the most devoted ones even bring fruits. They place these offerings in front of the god they worship and leave the incense to the professional incense watchers, who kindle the joss sticks for them. The prayers would give some incense coins, the amount of which ranges from one yuan, two yuan and five yuan, to ten yuan and fifty yuan, and hand in their names to the incense watcher (men give their family name as well as the first name; women give the family name of both her husband and herself; most of the prayers are housewives) and tell him what they are wishing for. The incense watcher moves the incense coins around the burning joss sticks for a couple of rounds and tells the gods how much the coins are worth before reporting to the gods about the prayers' request.

会里的人看香预卜吉凶祸福，他们就会说，"你给俺打个香"。一般而言，香客们都带数把香、一些金银元宝、火纸以及一些糕点来到庙会上。讲究的香客还会带水果之类的到所要祈求的神灵面前，将元宝、火纸放在神前，将香交给专门看香的看香人，请他给点燃。然后撂点儿油钱，如一块、两块、五块、十块、五十块不等。打香的香客向看香人通报自己的来处和姓氏（男的通报姓名，女的通报婆家姓氏和娘家姓氏。一般而言，来烧香的农村家庭主妇更多一些），告诉看香人自己要求什么。看香人将打香人的油钱在神像前燃着的香上转两转，告诉神灵他们送来了多少油钱，然后根据打香人的请求向神灵通报。

（八）许娃娃、套娃娃、还娃娃

求子也是庙会上的一项重要内容。求子有两种形式：一种是在龙牌前边套娃娃，一种是向龙牌或者是送子老母或者是其他神灵许娃娃。套娃娃是一种比较奇特的仪式，一般在二月初六进行。据龙牌会里的女会头米秋改说：

过会的时候四面八方来的神仙来祝寿，他们要讨论很多问题，清理很多赊账，但不包括套娃娃这本账。过了初六，这些神仙手头的账就上去了。所以，初六神仙手头的账清了，这才开始有时间照应套娃娃这件事。套娃娃这本账和其他账不是一本账，所以，一般都在初六这一天集中套娃娃。①

龙牌会里的人们准备了很多用黑线穿着的钱币，想要套娃娃的香客先在龙牌前边烧了香磕了头，跟龙牌爷说清楚是求男还是求女，许个愿，然

---

① 访谈对象：米秋改；访谈人：王均霞；访谈地点：赵县范庄龙祖殿；访谈时间：2010年4月13日。

h.Praying for More Babies

People also pray for more babies on temple fairs. There are two forms of this ceremony: one way is called "collecting baby coins", the other is to pray for babies to the Goddess of Birth or other gods. Collecting baby coins is a unique ritual, which is held on February 6th. According to Mi Qiugai, the female head of Dragon Tablet Club, the reason for holding the ceremony on this day is as follows:

When the Club ceremony is held on that day, gods from far and near would come to celebrate the birthday of the Dragon God and discuss many matters concerning mortals. They have to settle a variety of issues on credit with people, not including "collecting baby coins". On the sixth day, the issues are all solved, which leaves plenty of time for the gods to meet people's wishes for more babies. Therefore, the praying event often takes place on that day. ①

Members in Dragon Tablet Club put strings of coins together with black threads in advance. Firstly, prayers burn the joss sticks and kowtow in front of the Dragon Tablet; then they make a wish about whether they want a baby boy or baby girl; thirdly, they pick up the string of coins with three long joss

---

①Interviewee：Mi Qiugai；Interviewer：Wang Junxia；Place of interview：Dragon Ancestor Hall of Fanzhuage in Zhao County；Time of interview：April 13th, 2010.

sticks and rub it against the carved letters on the Tablet. The coin sticking to the letters during this process represents the baby that the gods promise. The host of the ritual gives a name to the baby, and the prayer heads for home with the lucky coin. He should not look back or talk on his way home, and as soon as he arrives home, he takes the coin immediately to the bedroom of the couple and put it up there. It is said to be a very effective way to have babies as people wish.

Whether it is "collecting baby coins" or "praying for more babies", the prayers must return to the Dragon Tablet Club with the one-month-old newly born baby if their wishes come true. They only bring one baby to the Club as it is the rule not to return with more babies than you have prayed. In addition, the prayer would ask the man who hosted the previous baby-praying ceremony for him to host the baby-returning baby ceremony. No mistakes should be made during the whole process as it is believed that babies must pay a visit to where they come from.

i.Sweeping the Hall

During the temple fair time, parents come to sweep the hall with their children. The ritual means

后拿三炷长香挑着穿着钱币的线头在龙牌上的字之间来回划拉，能得子的钱币很容易就能粘到龙牌上的字上面。这个钱就代表着娃娃。粘上以后，套娃娃这一仪式的主持人给孩子起个名字，求子的人就拿着这个铜钱往回走，一路上不能回头，也不能说话，回到家把这枚铜钱挂到夫妻俩的房间里。据说，这个套娃娃特别灵验。

不论是套娃娃还是许娃娃，如果求娃娃的香客回去之后果真如愿生子，那么在孩子满月之后就要来龙牌会上还娃娃。现在龙牌会上还娃娃的都还一个，求一命还一命，求了一个孩子就还回一个孩子，不能求了一个还回好几个，这样是乱了规矩。另外，得子的香客来还娃娃的时候，还得找当年为他们主持求子仪式的人主持还娃娃的仪式。同时，娃娃是在哪里求的还得在哪里还，不能出差错。

（九）扫堂

庙会期间，也有一些家长带着孩子到会上来扫堂。扫堂是一项标志着寄养在庙里的孩子不需要神灵给照应的仪式。在范庄以及周边村庄，一些人家的孩子是从龙牌会上求的，父母一般都会把这样的孩子寄养在庙里，请神给照应着。也有不是在庙里求的孩子，但一直身体羸弱，父母也将孩子寄养在庙里，请神给照应。寄养在庙里的孩子，每年父母都领着孩子到庙里系一个锁，就是一个用深蓝色穿着的钱币，一直系到孩子十二岁，就算孩子成人了。当孩子十二岁的时候，母亲就领着孩子到庙上扫堂。

扫堂的时候，父母要准备一个簸箕、一把笤帚、一方毛巾和一些香纸元宝，并让孩子带上所有的锁来到神前。在仪式主持人的指导下，孩子跪在神像前，双手合十，眼睛用带来的毛巾蒙上。仪式主持人拿笤帚在神像前和孩子身上来回扫，边扫边唱《扫堂歌》①：

that children fostered in the temple are ready to go on without the gods' protection. In Fanzhuang and villages around, thanks to the parents' praying, some children are born in the temple and they will stay and grow up in that temple under the protection of gods. Children with a weak body are also sent to the temple for gods' blessing. Parents of a temple-fostered child take him or her to the temple every year to tie a lock there, which is a coin threaded by a deep blue string, until the child is twelve years old. The child is considered a grown-up at this age, and it is time for the mother to take him or her to sweep the hall.

When sweeping the hall, the parents carry a dustpan, a broom, a towel and some papers as well as gold or silver ingots to the hall, and the child comes with all of his or her lucky locks. In the guidance of the host, the child kneels down in front of the statues of gods with his or her eyes covered by the towel. The host sweeps the floor in front of statues and claps the child with the broom, while chanting the *Hall Sweeping Ballad*:[1]

Your mother sent you to the gods' hall to make sure you grow up safe and sound.

You grow up with food from the gods, but you can no longer stay in the temple.

The towel weaved with white and blue threads are ready for you.

Let me cover it on your face, my naughty child, though it is not a costly gift.

Dustpan, my dustpan, made of wickers to bring you the wealth.

It is filled with gold, silver and treasures, though it is merely made of wickers.

The broom has five branches, nine ramie-wrapped branches bundled for ten times.

Let me sweep for my naughty boy with it, though it is not a costly gift. I sweep the east where the Eight Immortals attended the birthday celebration.

你娘哪怕你个不成人，把你哪寄到了佛家门，把你哟寄到了佛爷家哟门呀嗨。

从小哪吃的是佛家饭，长大哪不是呀佛家人，长大哟，不是咱佛爷家哟，人呀嗨。

这条哪手巾呀织得长，白线哪蓝线个织停当，白线哟蓝线个织也停哟当呀嗨。

虽说哪不是个知天的宝，蒙在哪顽童你头上，蒙在哟顽童哪你呀头哟上呀嗨。

簸箕儿仙哪个簸箕儿仙，簸箕哪本是个柳条编簸箕哟本是哪柳呀条哟，编呀嗨。

虽说哪不是个值钱的宝，金银哪财宝它往上端，金银哟财宝它往呀上哟端呀嗨。

这个哪笤帚它五道苗，九道哪麻经它扎十道，九道哟麻经它扎呀十哟道呀嗨。

虽说哪不是个知天的宝，俺给哪顽童把堂扫，俺给哟顽童你把也堂哟扫呀嗨。

东扫哪八仙个来上寿，西扫哪唐僧个来取经，西扫哟唐僧个来也去哟经呀嗨。

南扫哪老母个佛三家，北扫哪药王个和药圣，北扫哟药王个和药也哟圣呀嗨。

上扫哪青天个无遮挡，下扫哪地狱个十八层，下扫哟地狱个十也八哟层呀嗨。

上扫哪君来个下扫臣，扫扫哪顽童个这个人，扫扫哟顽童个这也个哟人呀嗨。

扫扫哪头上个明似镜，扫扫哪身上个无灾星，扫扫哟身上个无也灾哟星呀嗨。

扫扫哪前心个扫后心，扫你哪顽童个站住根，扫你哟顽童个站也住哟根呀嗨。

佛家哪保你个九十岁，一十哪二岁个出堂门，一十哟二岁个出也堂哟门呀嗨。

剪子哪打开个无钢锁，笤帚哪疙瘩个打出门，笤帚哟疙瘩个打也出哟门呀嗨。

I sweep the west where Tangsen the Monk headed for a pilgrimage to the Buddhist scriptures.

I sweep the south where the Three Goddesses of White Lotus live. I sweep the north where the God of Medicine and Doctor Sun Simiao live.

I sweep the heaven above our head and the hell beneath the ground.

I sweep the Emperor as well as his ministers, and sweep you, my naughty child.

I sweep your smart mind and your healthy body and bad luck will stay away.

I sweep all the corners of your heart and nothing evil will take you away.

The gods' blessings protect you for nine to ten years, now you are leaving on your twelfth year.

Scissors cut off the locks and brooms send you out of the hall.

When the host sings out the word "scissors", people cut off the lock-necklace around the child 's neck and place it in front of the statues of gods; the child run out of the hall and the host throw the broom out of the door, too. And this is the end of the Hall Sweeping ceremony, which marks the growing up of the child. The child is allowed to take part in all kinds of ancestor worshiping activities from then on.

j.Drama Performances

For people in Fanzhuang, a temple fair is never a good one without Chinese opera performance. Nominally the operas are performed to entertain the gods. Every year on Dragon Tablet Club ceremony, opera troupes are invited to give performances. In early years, the performances are often given by local troupes and last a long time. During 1970s to 1980s, two performing troupes would start at the same time, and people could choose to watch whichever they preferred. The opera stage is set up on an opening not far away from the Dragon Tablet Club. When temple fairs are held, performing troupes are busy setting the stage, and old men and women carry the stools from their houses to take up the best positions and wait in amusement. People from other villages to take part in the temple affair are gathered under the stage to enjoy themselves; some even come all the way just for the opera performance. Therefore, before the performance begins, there are already crowds of people waiting in front of the stage, most

等到唱到"剪子"那一句的时候，人们将孩子脖子上的锁剪开，扔在神像前，孩子开始往外跑，主持人则将笤帚用力扔向大门外。这样，扫堂的仪式基本就结束了。这标志着孩子成人了，以后可以去参加祭祖之类的活动了。

（十）唱戏

对于范庄人来说，"没有戏就不叫庙会"，这些戏名义上是给神唱的。因此，每年龙牌会过会的时候，都会请戏班子来唱戏。早些年都是请当地的戏班子来唱，唱的场数也比较多。上世纪七八十年代，有一年请了两台戏同时唱，谁爱去看什么就去看什么。范庄村的戏台就搭在离龙牌会不远的一块空地上，每到庙会的时候，戏班子的人将戏台收拾好。范庄村的老头老婆们就从家里拿了板凳，在戏台下边占好位子，津津有味地看。许多来赶庙会的外村人，也过来看热闹。有些人还是专门赶过来听戏的，因此，戏一开演，戏台下面就聚集了很多人。看戏的以老头儿老太太居多，从远处看过去，基本都是深蓝色中山装和白头巾，很有河北特色。

（十一）集市

庙会期间，周边村落的商贩也纷纷赶到范庄来赶庙会。龙祖殿前的热闹和龙祖殿外的热闹交相辉映，让庙会期间的范庄节日气氛格外浓郁。范庄的集市就在龙祖殿东边那条宽阔的水泥路上，平时逢五、逢十在这条路上逢集，但由于范庄周围也有不少集市，所以平时集市上人并不多。但是，庙会期间，集市上人潮涌动，非常热闹。集市上的商品主要以日常生产生活用品以及家用电器等为主，尤以吃食为多。各种水果如苹果、香蕉、菠萝等占据了集市的很大空间，各种糕点、干果也是庙会上的主要商品。吃饭摊子也布满了整个集市。吃饭摊子基本上都是现做现卖。每天早上八九点，做小吃生意的商贩来到这条街道

of whom are old couples. Seen from distance, it is a sea of dark blue Chinese tunic suits and white headscarves.

k. Markets

Businessmen and retailers come from neighbor villages also take part in the temple fairs. The bustling crowds can be seen everywhere, as festival atmosphere can be felt both in front of the Dragon Ancestor Hall and outside the hall. The market of Fanzhuang is set on the broad cement road in east of the hall on the fifth day and tenth day of every month. As it isn't the only market in the area, the market is never crowded on workdays; but during the temple fairs, it attracts a great many visitors and customers. Goods on the market are mainly commodities for daily use and household appliances, especially food. There are all kinds of fruits, such as

apples, bananas and pineapples as well as various cakes and cookies and nuts. Snack booths can be seen everywhere in the temple fairs. At eight or nine o'clock in the morning, snack retailers are ready for their customers with booths and cookers set up.

The road extending from east to west behind the Dragon Ancestor Hall is also a perfect market for the retailers, most of whom are selling incense papers, cookies and snacks. Further along the street are cloth booths, where the cloth is not sold by pieces but by jin (1/2 kilogram). Turn to the north end of the road, you can still see the booths of cloth, including the materials for making the tiger-head shoes. Go further along the road, and you can see an indoor market with lines of clothes shops. On the south of the market is an opening, which used to be a playground for children. In addition, there are also a lot of toys for children, such as models of knives, guns and sticks, and colorful balloons, which are very popular among these young customers.

4. Conclusion

As a public holiday activity for Fanzhuang Village, Dragon Tablet Club celebration is closely related to the daily life of local people. During the

上，开始搭棚并将炉灶支好，等待客人的到来。

龙祖殿后面那条东西向的路上也布满了商摊，这一块以卖香纸和作为供品的小点心为主。再往里走是卖布头的，布头不是论块卖，而是论斤称。这条路走到头，拐弯向北，仍然以卖布料的为主，在这里可以见到比较有特色的做虎头鞋的料子，再往前走是一个搭起了棚的市场，里面一排一排全是卖衣服的。这个市场南边还有一块空地，在庙会期间，这里就是一个游乐场，是小孩子的乐园。另外，庙会上也有很多小孩子的玩意儿，比如刀枪棍棒，以及五颜六色的氢气球等，很是吸引小孩子的目光。

四、结语

范庄龙牌会作为范庄村公共性的节日活动，它与当地的日常生活紧密地联系到了一起。在二月二龙牌会期间，颇具特色的"游龙仪式"、锣鼓喧天的花会表演、二月初二晚上的焰火、龙祖殿外的坠子戏、热闹的集市，着实让范庄民众沉浸在节日的热闹和欢乐里。龙牌会也为当地民众提供了一个健身娱乐的场所。每当秧歌扭起来、锣鼓敲起来的时候，参与者脸上洋溢着的灿烂笑容，说明他们在这样的活动中得到了乐趣，旁观的民众也同样获得了满足。近几年，龙牌会的规模越办越大，借着学者和新闻媒体的宣传，龙牌会为更多的人所了解。这些既为当地带来了商机，也提高了赵县的知名度。显然，龙牌会已经成为当地文化的一张响当当的名片。

celebration on February 2nd, there are the unique Dragon Tablet Marching rituals, the magnificent folk arts performances, fireworks on the evening of February 2nd, opera performances outside the Dragon Ancestor Hall and busy markets, all of which breathe the joyous and lively air into people's life and provide an occasion for local villagers to entertain themselves physically and mentally. In the paces of Yangko Dances and the sounds of drums and cymbals, people both taking part in the performance and watching aside are inspired and satisfied with smiles on their faces. Dragon Table Club has grown in size and scale in recent years; as a result of the media publicity and scholars' promotion, it is known by more and more people. The fame brings business opportunities for local people while making Zhao County a well-known cultural destination for travelers. Apparently, Dragon Tablet Club becomes the brand of local culture.

3 鲁北"娃娃会"
Clay-made Baby Fair in Northern Shangdong

Torch Li Village of Huimin County in Shandong Province holds an annual grand temple fair on February 2nd of lunar year. The lovely and delicate Henan Zhang clay-made babies attract a large number of visitors and prayers in the temple fair, especially women who have no children after being married. They rush to buy for themselves one or two of the "babies", which is called "gaining babies". Therefore, the temple fair in this area on that day is also called "Clay-made Baby Fair".

1. The Torch Li Village in Huimin County

Torch Li Village has a population less than eight hundred and lies on an alluvial plain whose formation is due to the Yellow River's changing of routes. The low-lying lands in the village are saline-alkali soil unfavorable for growing crops;

在山东省惠民县火把李村，每年农历二月二日都会举行盛大的庙会活动。庙会上最抢眼的物品要数形态各异、漂亮可爱的河南张泥娃娃，吸引着大量的香客，尤其是那些婚后不育的妇女前来购买，谓之"拴娃娃"。因此，火把李二月二庙会又叫"娃娃会"。

一、走进惠民火把李

火把李是一个人口不足八百的小村庄，地处黄河改道或决口的河间地带，由静水沉积而成。村中地貌多为浅平洼地，土壤以盐碱地为主，不适宜农作物生长，村民生计条件比较艰苦。在村民的记忆中，火把李村曾经历了一段艰难的开荒历史。以前，村子四周全是白光光的碱场地，播种的庄稼长不出来，只长些芦草。人走在上面，鞋底会踩得成白色的。过了二月二后，人们就开始忙着浇地、耕地、种棉花，种了后因为是碱场地，人们还得补苗，有的要补好几遍，好地有八成苗，碱场地有六成苗。种麦子的时候每年种三四遍都没有多少苗。人们以前称碱场地为兔子不拉屎的地方。以前因为穷，若是外村的闺女要往这庄里说亲，家人就会调侃说上那兔子都不拉屎的地方干什么啊，没有吃的，也没有烧的。经过几代人的努力，近几年村里的地逐渐都得到了改良。

火把李是个杂姓村，有崔、王、李、刘等姓氏。崔姓是本地人，也是最早来村的立地户，比村里皇姑庙的修建时间还要早，有"先有崔家坟，后

as a result, life of villagers is extremely hard. In the past, villagers have gone through a difficult time of cultivating the virgin land, when there were only alkali soils in the village and weeds in the field. A walk in the fields would leave your shoes with white soles as the saline-alkali soil was sticked to them. After February 2nd, people were busy with irrigation and cultivation, but they had to be re-seeding for several times because of the bad condition of soil. Better lands could survive eighty percent of the seedlings while saline-alkali soil could only afford sixty percent seedlings. Very few seedlings of wheat could survive even it is re-planted for three or four times. Therefore, saline-alkali lands in this village was called a place where even filthy swine despise, referring to poverty of the village and infertility of its lands, that was why people in neighbor villages won't marry their daughters to young men of this village. In recent years, with efforts of generations, the situation is improved.

There are more than one family name in Torch Li Village, such as Cui, Wang, Li and Liu. People of the family name Cui are the first settlers in this village, earlier than the building of Temple of Emperor Sister, as a saying goes like this, "The grave of Cui family are years older than that of

Temple of Emperor Sister". People of other families, such as Liu, Li, Zhao and Wang were migrated from Zaoqiang County in Hebei Province. The name of the village has been changed for several times, the stories of these changes are told by oral history till today. It is said that in earlier times when the village was just set, there was a Temple of Evergreen near the village, so it was named Evergreen Temple at first. Later, when wars began, lots of soldiers died and were buried here, and will-o'-the-wisp of corpse sparkling in shape of torches was often seen in the field near the house of Li family. So when the Evergreen Temple was pulled down, the village changed its name to Torch Li. And the villagers' own explanation is as follows:

The wildfires in the field were from the bones and skeletons of people killed in the battlefield. It is the phosphorescent light as phosphorus would self-ignite at the temperature of 34 degree centigrade. There used to be foxes running with "fires" burning on their furs, which is also the trick of phosphorus. Where did the phosphorus on the "burning fur" come from? Because the fox would love to squeeze through the holes in the wet underground and come out with phosphorus around its body. When it came out, the phosphorus rubbed with the air and caught fire. As a result, there were wildfires jumping everywhere in the fields. Sometimes it was not the foxes that carried the fires, the fires jumped and flashed themselves when the air rose and fell, as the phosphorus is very light in weight. The phenomenon

有皇姑庙"之说。其他的刘、李、赵、王姓都是元朝末年由河北省枣强县迁居于此。该村的村名几经变革，至今还流传着许多传说。早在立村之初，村旁有一座长春寺，因此村名也曾叫长春寺。后来，此地战争频发，丧生于这一带的军卒很多，入夜常见磷光闪闪，状如火把，位置又是在姓李的户家那边，故在长春寺拆除后，村名叫了一阵李王庄后又改称火把李。对此，村民有自己的解释：

这些火的来源就是过去战场上的那些人的骨头，其实就是磷火。那些骨头年数多了就产生磷吗，磷到摄氏34℃开始自燃。原来那个狐狸叫"火皮子"，跑起来后看着身上有火，也烧不着它的毛，其实就是那个磷火在着。"火皮子"身上那些磷是哪来的呢？就是它经常在地底下来回地钻，带出一些磷来。它一出来跑，和空气摩擦，就着火了。这里满地里蹦跶到处都是火，当然并不都是狐狸。磷很轻，稍微有点空气波动它就会蹦跶，村南、村北都是这个样。因为这个事就把李王庄改名为火把李了，好像村中周围都是火把一样。

虽然生活在较为贫瘠的土地上，物质条件并不好，但火把李村有着自己的传统娱乐活动。比如正月里有"闹灯节"，村民自发组织起来，踩高跷、跑秧歌，十分热闹。另外就是每年二月二举行的火把李庙会了，这是该村一年一度的香火会、买卖会和狂欢节。用村民自己的话说，就是每逢这天家家户户就像过年一样，二月二相当于过了第二遍年。

二、没有庙的庙会

火把李村曾有皇姑庙、团圆宫、关帝庙、小关帝庙、三义庙、土地庙等六座庙宇，其中皇姑庙是村里最大的庙宇，庙中的皇姑是掌管生育之神，关系着家庭生活的命运。团圆宫供奉的是皇姑的家人，象征着亲人的团圆。

was observed both in the north and south of the village. Thus the name Li Wang Village was changed into Torch Li Village; it is as if the village is surrounded by torches.

Though life is not easy in this village due to the infertile lands, Torch Li Village has its own traditional, recreational activities, such as the Lantern Day in January, when villagers organize themselves to perform stilts walking and Yangko Dancing. Another one is the temple fair on February 2nd in Torch Li Village, which is the annual praying assembly, buying-and-selling fair and carnival day. According to the villagers, it is like reviving the Spring Festival Day again on February 2nd.

2.A Temple Fair without Temple

There used to be six temples in Torch Li Village: the Temple of Emperor Sister, the Temple of Reunion, the Temple of Lord Guanyu, the Guarding Temple of Lord Guanyu, the Temple of Three Righteousness and the Temple of the God of Earth. The Temple of Emperor Sister is the largest temple in the village; Emperor Sister, the Goddess of reproduction, is in charge of the family life. The family members of Emperor Sister is enshrined in the Temple of Reunion, indicating a happy family reunion. The two temples of Lord Guanyu and the Temple of God of Earth are respectively built for General Guanyu famous for his loyalty in history and for the God of Earth, hoping that they would bless the villagers and guard the village. The grand temple fair in Torch Li Village was held to show respect to gods in the six temples in the past; today, none of the temples is maintained, and we can only imagine their prosperity from the narrations of the elders in the village. However, the temple fair is celebrated by generations. The joyous crowds and the bustling streets still maintain the glorious scene of the old days. Liu Hongmu, one of the villagers, proudly told us that the practice of the temple fair was never suspended, not in snowing or raining days, nor in the Cultural Revolution when many traditions were abolished.

"When I was old enough to remember things, I can recall that the temple fair is very prosperous. The streets were filled with people on February 2nd. One day about fifteen years ago, it was snowing heavily, yet people still came to the temple fair in the deep snow. If people failed to come on February 2nd, they would come on the next day, when the temple fair was less crowded. It was never interrupted, and people living nearby within forty li all came to it. At that time, even when officials from the County tried to stop people from going to it, they

大小关帝庙和土地庙则分别为祭祀关公和土地爷而建，希望他们保佑一方平安。正是在以皇姑庙为中心的庙宇群落的基础上，形成了声势浩大的火把李庙会。现如今，火把李村中的庙宇早已荡然无存，我们只能从村里老人的口述中来推测当时庙宇的盛况。然而，庙虽不存，火把李庙会顽强地传承下来了，拥挤的人群、热闹的集市，仍然延续着当年庙会的繁华景象。村民刘洪木向我们自豪地回忆说，庙会从来没有间断过，无论是遇到下雪天还是雨天，哪怕是在"文化大革命"破四旧、立四新时，庙会也没有停过。

"从我记事起，庙会就很兴旺。二月二这天出门就看到很多人，十分拥挤。有一年，大概是15年前，下着大雪，人们仍然踩着很深的积雪来赶庙会。有的人二月二来不了，二月初三也会来补上。不过初三时人就很少了，但是庙会总是灭不了（方言，中断不了）。

四十里之内的人们都来这里……那时县里、乡里的干部在路口截着不让赶会，撵得人们到处跑，但是人们就是绕道也是偷偷地来。"①

可见，无论自然环境和社会环境如何变化，火把李庙会都以其旺盛的生命力延续着，这既是当地民众出于自身需要的自发选择，也说明了传统庙会在民间社会具有深厚的根基。

三、泥塑

早上7点来钟，庙会上的人已经很多，从上午8点到中午12点左右，整个庙会上人山人海，拥挤如潮，热闹非凡。一直到傍晚时分，庙会上的人们仍然络绎不绝，整个村落都沉浸在一种节日的喜庆气氛中，村民们和周围村落的民众都热情高涨地来赶会，彰显出乡土社会中人们强烈的年节意识。

① 被访谈人：刘洪木，访谈人：邓霞，访谈时间：2007年3月20日，访谈地点：火把李村刘连文家。

still took a detour to sneak to the site of the temple fair."①

From the above description, we can see that the temple fair in Torch Li Village has a vigorous vitality in spite of the change of natural and social environment, thanks to local people's lasting passion towards it and the deep-rooted tradition that gives birth to its popularity.

3.Clay Figurines

At about seven o'clock in the morning, there are already a lot of people gathered in the temple fair. From eight o'clock to the midday, people are swarming to the temple fair and the street is crowded with exciting and noisy visitors. At dusk, more people come to the fair as the whole village is bathed in happy festival air. Villages and their neighbor nearby are all filled with enthusiasm, which shows a strong consciousness of traditional festival in villagers' minds.

①Interviewee: Liu Hongmu, Interviewer: Deng Xia, Time of Interview: March 20th, 2007, Place of Interview: The house of Liu Lianwen, Torch Li Village

"Henan Zhang, the village faces the south gate; every house in the village is good at making clay figurines." One of the features of Torch Li Temple Fair is the Henan Zhang clay figurines. Henan Zhang is a village well-known for its clay figurines. There is a beautiful legend about the history of the clay craft there. It is said that in 1426, Zhu Gaoxu, Prince Han of Ming Dynasty (son of Zhu Di, the Emperor of chengzu, and uncle of Zhu Zhanji, Emperor of xuanzong), decided to rebel in his manorin Le'an (Huimin County). He ordered to mold weapons, and local young men were forced to join the army. Livestock and grains were taken away from farms and people were complaining. One day, an elegant old Taoist priest came to Henan Zhang

"河南张，朝南门，家家户户捏泥人。"说到火把李庙会，不能不提及河南张泥塑。河南张是当地的一个村子，以制作泥塑而闻名。关于泥塑的来历，民间传颂着一个美丽的传说。据说，明宣德元年（1426年）汉王朱高煦（明成祖朱棣之子，明宣宗朱瞻基的叔叔）据乐安州（今惠民县）图谋叛乱，广造兵器，在当地抓壮丁，夺民畜、粮草，人们怨声载道。一天，河南

张村来了一位鹤发童颜的老道宣称："……捏成九千九百九十九个泥人，待九九八十一天，张天师来作法，使泥人成为天兵天将，灭高煦，救民于苦难。"于是，全村男女老少，昼夜和泥捏人。可巧泥人做成，九九八十一天，宣宗皇帝御驾亲征，朱高煦事败被缚，当地人民免于苦难。泥人虽未变成天兵，但乡民们视之为吉祥物，争相购买。从此，祖辈沿袭至今。

火把李庙会是一个泥娃娃的盛会，会上出售的泥娃娃大都来自河南张村。以前这个庙会叫香火会，村中曾有多处庙宇，香火很盛。当地有到庙会上"拴娃娃"的风俗，已婚妇女如果数年不生育，就会拿着一根线到庙上去祭拜神仙，然后到集市上买泥娃娃，用红色的细绳拴在小泥娃娃的脖子上带回家，俗信这样就能生育了。来庙会求子拴娃娃的以老婆婆和小媳妇居多。在过去那个泥土里刨食的年代，拥有下田收粮的壮

Village and told the villagers, "If you make 9,999 clay figurines and invite Master Zhang (a famous wizard) to play magic on the figurines, they will turn into gallant soldiers and defeat Zhu Gaoxu to save all of you." The villagers did as the priest told them. Men and women, old and young, all started to make clay figurines day and night; on the 81st day, Emperor Xuanzong arrived with his army and Zhu Gaoxu was defeated and arrested. The local people were rescued from their misery. Though the clay figurines never turned into soldiers from heaven, villagers nearby all considered them as a symbol of luck and made panic purchase of them. From then on, the craft was passed down by generations of villagers of Henan Zhang till today.

Torch Li Temple Fair is a great exhibition for the clay figurines, most of which are produced from Henan Zhang village. The temple fair used to be called temple fair of incense burning, as there were many temples in the village and a lot of prayers came to offer the sacrifice. There is a custom of "gaining babies" on the temple fair. If a married woman cannot get pregnant, she will come to pray to the gods in the temple with a red string in hand and buy a clay-made baby figurine in the temple fair. She ties the red string around the neck of the figurine and takes it home; in this way, it is believed that she will soon have a baby. Most of the prayers coming to the temple fair to "gain babies" are grannies and young wives. In the old days when people made a living by growing food in the earth, strong male laborers for farm work is the hope of

every family in the countryside. Newly married women would be praised by the husband's family by having given birth to baby boys. This custom may explain why Torch Li Village Temple Fair can enjoy such popularity for so many years.

劳力是每家每户最热切的希望。家有男丁意味着香火绵延，小媳妇也会因为儿子的降生而获得婆家的赞许和荣誉。这可能是火把李庙会经久不衰的重要原因。

4.Buying and Selling

In the past, goods for sale in temple fair of Torch Li Village were tools for production and daily life, such as baskets, toys, cattails-made cushions, spinning machines, pickaxes and woods for house making. According to the elders in the village, businesses on temple fair day were often better than those on normal market day, so it was also called a day for "buying and selling". In today's temple fair, besides a variety of time-honored clay figurines

四、买卖会

以前的火把李庙会上主要卖条子筐、玩具、蒲墩子、纺车子、大镐、锨、盖屋的木头等生产生活工具。据村里的老人讲，庙会这天做买卖的生意很好，平时的集市就没有庙会这天好，所以也叫"买卖会"。如今的庙会上，除了传承久远、每年都有各种各样的泥娃娃、各种生活用品和生产工具，还有各种杂耍游戏，儿童玩具模型组合，民间艺人扎的灯笼、葫芦；也活跃着一些写水笔画的艺人、卖古玩的和为庆祝庙会在村里现场演出的几个歌舞团等。有的人从40里之外的商河县、阳信县、无棣县、广饶县赶来，还有远道而来的各大媒体的记者、摄影爱好者和民俗爱好者。学者的询问、各大媒体的镜头也成为当今庙会的一大景观。正是，地方的民众、政府部门、媒体、文化人、文化团体、小商贩等，共同营造当代庙会文化的氛围，这是该地区一场"全民性的活动"。

and tools for production and daily life every year, there are also many game exhibitions, toy models for children, lanterns, bottle gourds and brush paintings made by folk artists, antique sales and live performances of singing and dancing troupes in the village. Some people come all the way from Shanghe County, Yangxin County, Wudi County and Guangrao County about 40 *li* away. Journalists, photographers, folk-custom amateurs and scholars all take part in this grand ceremony, which is the focus of media and even becomes a part of the temple fair. The cultural atmosphere is created by the joint efforts from local public, authorities, media, intellectuals, cultural organizations and retailers; it becomes an activity of all people.

5. Visiting Relatives

It is a common practice in Torch Li Village that married women go back to her parents' house and pay a visit to her family grave three days before the temple fair, which is believed to be a gesture of inviting the dead ones in her family to take part in the temple fair. On the temple fair day, relatives who are too busy to pay a visit to each other come to Torch Li Village from nearby villages to call on their relatives while enjoying the temple fair. Villagers in Torch Li Village entertain their guests with delicious dinners. There are also some sayings related to home coming in the village, such as "married daughters visit their mothers on February 2nd", and "on February 2nd when dragon raises its head, parents greet their home-coming daughters and listen to their complaints about marriage and life". Some villagers would go to pick up their aged relatives or daughters to the temple fair.

Therefore, the temple fair makes February 2nd of Torch Li village the day of reception. It is "Women's Day" and "Children's Day" for women and kids in neighboring villages, the Expo Day for folk arts such as Henan Zhang clay figurines, and a memorial day for countryside markets. Temple fairs provide women with a relaxing time and encourage the children to enjoy their playful nature; they also satisfy the urban dwellers' desire for country life and give glory and honor to Torch Li Village. The practice of temple fair meets the various needs of different groups of people, which leads to its popularity and longevity.

五、走亲戚

火把李村祖祖辈辈传下来的讲究是，外嫁的妇女须在庙会的前三天回娘家上坟。按照村民的说法，就是上坟邀请去世的亲人也来赶会。每逢庙会这天，春节期间来不及走动的亲戚都从周边村落赶来火把李，既是赶庙会，也是走亲戚。火把李村村民准备好酒菜，热情招待。此外，村里还有"二月二走娘家"、"二月二龙抬头，家家接女诉冤愁"等说法。有的村民会提前一两天去接上了岁数的亲戚或是"老闺女"来赶会。

可见，因为庙会，火把李的二月二已经成为远客近亲的"接待日"。它是四邻八乡的"妇女节"，是小娃娃大孩子的"儿童节"，是河南张泥塑等乡土艺术的"博览会"，又是乡村集市的"纪念日"。庙会提供了妇女的休憩权利，顺应了儿童的游戏天性，满足了都市人的乡土情怀，赋予了火把李村以荣誉感。能够满足不同人群的本性需

要，使得火把李庙会的天时地利人和，古老的庙会因此而长盛不衰。

4 鲁南"峄山会"
Temple Fair of Mount Yishan in Southern Shandong

在山东省邹城市东南12公里处，有一座著名的山峰，叫作峄山。峄山是一座富有灵气的神山，山上庙宇众多，有送子娘娘庙（即子孙石）、玉皇大殿、泰山老奶奶庙、小白庙、夫子洞、八仙洞等。在当地人的眼中，这些庙宇有求必应，非常灵验。秀美的自然风光、动听的神话传说和神圣的庙宇群落使得峄山成为当地的一处著名

About 12 kilometers away from the southeast of Zoucheng City in Shandong Province, there is a famous mount called Yishan. Mount Yishan is a holy mountain with many temples such as Temple of the Goddess of Reproduction, Jade Emperor Temple, Temple of the Old Lady of Mount Tai, Temple of Junior White, the Cave of Confucius and the Cave of the Eight Immortals. In the eyes of local people, gods living in these temples grant whatever is requested. The beautiful landscape, touching legends and stories and sacred temples make Mount Yishan one of the most attractive tourist destinations in this area and it is considered as a place embodying the essence of Shandong and connecting to the best part of Mount Tai with large numbers of prayers coming to worship the gods every year. On February 2nd, there is a grant temple fair where visitors from all over the area come to burn incense and worship the gods, which is a lively and noisy occasion with large crowds of people.

景观，有"邹鲁灵秀，灵通泰岱"的美誉，香火十分旺盛。每年的二月二日，这里都要举办声势浩大的庙会活动，吸引着四面八方的香客前来烧香祭拜，形成摩肩接踵的热闹场面。

1. The Origin of Temple Fair

一、庙会的起源

Temple Fair of Mount Yishan has a history of more than a thousand years. The origin of the temple fair was recorded in the *Chronicle of Mount Yishan*, "615 BC, Lord Zhuwen moved his capital to the north of Yishan, and celebrated the event on February 2nd that year after they settled there.

峄山庙会是一个有上千年历史的古会。关于庙会的起源，《峄山新志》载："公元前615年，邾文公卜迁于峄山之阳作国都，一切搬迁事宜妥当

后，第一个欢庆祝贺之日即二月初二日。自此，峄山每年二月二日有会，流传至今以作纪念。"①而在民间的传说故事中，却有另外一种解释：

有个八十多岁的老头，他每天都很勤快地耕地种田，并且也卖东西贴补家用。有一天，他发现一个葫芦，这个神奇的葫芦经常往外冒出东西，油盐酱醋、粮食等什么都有，于是他便把这些东西分给老百姓，日久天长，老百姓们就都学懒了，也不种地了。之后有一天，他做梦梦见街上很多人做买卖，卖什么的都有，日用品、杂货等。他醒来后，便号召村民在这天形成一个会，一是可以让老百姓有饭吃，二是可以改变他们的懒惰，而这天恰好是农历二月二。于是以后便形成了二月二庙会的传统。②

Since then, there were celebration activities on that day every year as a commemoration."[1] But in folk stories another explanation goes as follows:

Once there was an old man in his eighties, who was very diligent in farming every day and also sold goods. One day, he found a magic gourd on the road, which gave him all sorts of things such as oil, salts, sauce, vinegar and grains. He decided to share it with others. Day by day, people became lazier and lazier, so that they no longer did their farm work. Later, he dreamt that a lot of people on the street sold all kinds of things, including articles of daily use and groceries. When he woke up, he initiated a meeting on that day among the villagers in a purpose that people were free from hunger while getting rid of their laziness. The day was February 2nd, therefore, the practice of holding a temple fair on that day was passed down. [2]

---

①田振铎、刘玉平、秦显耀：《峄山新志》，济宁：济宁市新闻出版局，1993年，第210页。
②被访谈人：刘大爷，访谈人：张佳，访谈时间：2008年3月9日，访谈地点：峄山村大街。

①Tian Zhengduo, Liu Yuping, Qin Xianyao: *New Records of Yishan*, Jining: Press and Publication Bureau, 1993, p. 230.
②Interviewee: Grandpa Liu, Interviewer: Zhang Jia, Time of Interview: March 9th, 2008, Place of Interview: Street of Yishan Village

In fact, Mount Yishan Temple Fair is a religious meeting as well as a buying and selling fair. On that day, there would be large numbers of merchants coming to do business. The story above is based on the impression of the goods and materials exchange on February 2nd in people's mind, but it also reflects the important status that the temple fair occupies in people's life. The temple fair on February 2nd is a grand annual event, which attracts people from neighboring areas such as Zoucheng urban area, Jining, Xuzhou, Tengzhou and Fan County. Generally, the fair begins on February 1st, as retailers and traders arrange their booths on that day. Most people come on the second day and the third day. For people living around the temple fair site, the event is part of their life, and the day can never be counted as a festival day without buying a bowl of porridge and a "*Chunji*"[1] (a chicken-shaped, silk-made toy) from the temple fair and a trip to Mount Yishan. For married daughters grown up in this area, they often return to their parents' houses on February 2nd to visit their parents and to enjoy themselves in the temple fair. Besides their married

---

[1] *Chunji* (Spring chicken) is a popular toy and aircraft in Zoucheng and Zaozhuang, mainly on sale from the Beginning of Spring to March. *Chunji* in Zoucheng looks like a small bird. It is made of silk. This is the way to make it: firstly, bind up the straw from corn cobs with cottons to make the shape of a bird; then boil the silkworm cocoon with hot water and reel off the silk from the cocoons; the silk then is twined around the semifinished work to make more delicate shapes; the final step is to paste feathers on the tail and draw the other parts of the body with colorful pens. Most of the spring chicken are in red, green and yellow, which cater to the villagers' aesthetic standards.

事实上，峄山庙会既是香火会，又是买卖会，每逢庙会都有大批商客前来做生意。这则传说显然是当地人基于二月二庙会物资交流的直观想象而形成，但也说明了庙会在人们心目中的重要地位。每年的二月二日都热闹非凡，来赶会的人来自十里八乡乃至邹城市区，甚至有从济宁、徐州、滕州、范县等地赶来的。一般在二月初一便开始有会，买卖人已经开始布置摊位，二月二当天人最多，持续到二月初三。对附近的居民来说，二月二逛峄山庙会是他们难以割舍的生活，到庙会上喝一碗粥、买一只"春鸡"①、爬一爬峄山，才能算是过了节的。对于出嫁到别处的闺

---

① 春鸡是流传在邹城、枣庄等地的一种玩具和工艺品，主要在立春至二月二期间出售使用。邹城鹌鸡状如小鸟，主要材料为蚕丝。制作时，先做胎，以玉米棒秸为胎，用棉花缠胎，做出大体形状。然后用热水烫蚕，抽丝（缫丝）缠到胎上，进一步做出细致的形状。成形后，在尾巴上粘上鸡毛，最后用彩色颜料画上眼睛、羽毛、身子。春鸡的颜色多为红色、绿色和黄色等鲜艳的色彩，与乡民大红大绿的审美观协调一致。

女，二月二这一天常常会回娘家省亲。一是看望父母，二是来赶峄山会，图个热闹。除了闺女回娘家，也有许多其他的亲戚来做客。所以，峄山脚下的村民，每家每户在二月初一都会精心准备下饭菜，以招待二月二来做客的亲朋好友。这样一来，单纯的嫁女归宁习俗就逐渐演变成更为宽泛意义上的亲朋相聚。在这种氛围下的二月二节就显得格外热闹。

二、香火会

峄山上众多神圣的庙宇，以及灵验的传说故事，使得二月二这天的峄山庙会成为重要的香火会。香客上山进香有求平安的，有求生意兴隆的，还有求子的。峄山上的送母娘娘很是灵验，结了婚的妇女多来此烧香求子。送母娘娘是当地人对送子娘娘的俗称，过去峄山上曾有送母娘娘庙，庙前是寓意得子的子孙石。现庙

daughters, on February 2nd the villagers at the foot of Mount Yishan also receive many relatives in their house with well-prepared meals on the previous day. Thanks to the temple fair, the practice of married girls returning home becomes a family reunion of relatives and friends, which makes the Day of February 2nd more warm and exciting among local people.

2.Religious Meeting

There were various temples on Mount Yishan with legends, making the temple fair a significant religious meeting. Prayers go to the temple in Mount Yishan, some pray for life without mishap, some pray for a prosperous business, and others pray for more sons. The Goddess in charge of reproduction on Mount Yishan always grants the requests from the prayers, so married women often come to burn some joss sticks and pray for more children. The Goddess was used to be enshrined in the Temple of Goddess of Reproduction on the Mount Yishan, with a Stone of Offspring in front of it, which means more sons to the prayers. Now the temple has been torn down, but the Stone is still there.

Besides the prayers burning incenses in front of the Stone for more children, some prayers come to pray for fortune and show gratitude to the gods for satisfying their wish in front of Temple of the Supreme Deity of Taoism and Temple of Ling guan, other prayers come to climb the mount for sightseeing on this festival occasion, where they could stay away from the busy work and life, and enjoy the traditional, joyous atmosphere in the temple fair with their hearts greatly satisfied.

3.Buying and selling

Buying and selling activities on Yishan Temple Fair mostly take place on the main road towards Mount Yishan. Several hundreds of booths are set

已拆毁，仅存子孙石。

除了子孙石前烧香求子的香客，在玉皇大帝庙、灵官庙前也都有众多的香客来求吉还愿；另有许多人只是以节日的名义来登山游览，远离紧张的工作与生活节奏，体验庙会上那种传统吉祥的热闹氛围，获得一种心灵的满足感。

三、买卖会

峄山庙会上的买卖活动主要集中在通往峄山的一条主道上，几百家摊位在路两旁整齐排列，从峄山的大门口一直延伸到山脚下，十分壮观。商品的种类有农具、生活用品、食品、文化商品、游艺、玩具等。在改革开放前，每逢峄山会，县里会传达命令，周边乡镇的供销社都要来赶会，进行商品买卖。由此可见，在交通和信息都相对不发达的时代，物资交流是峄山庙会的主要内容。二月正是春耕开始的时节，各种农具和农资可以通过二月二庙会来买卖，村民可以借此机会备齐春耕所需的农具设备，同时庙会上众多的买卖种类也满足了人们日常对于生活用品的各种需求。

现在随着生活水平的提高，各个村子都有超市，加上交通方便，大家随时都可以买到生产生活用品，庙会上卖的基本上都是吃的和玩的，大多迎合小孩子的兴趣。庙会物资交流的作用减弱，更多的是体现休闲娱乐的功能。峄山上的客流量在二月二这天达到顶峰，前来上香祭拜和观

in lines along the road, stretching from the gate to the foot of Mount Yishan in a spectacular sight. The category of goods ranges from agricultural tools, articles for daily use, food, cultural products and toys. Before the drive of reform and opening up, when Yishan Temple Fair is held, orders from the county would ask all of the supplying and marketing agencies to take part in the event and join the transaction activities. It can be seen that in the time when transportation and information exchanges were not so convenient, goods and materials exchanges made the main content of the temple fair. February is the month when spring farming begins, as all kinds of farming tools and materials are exchanged in Yishan Temple Fair, and villagers take this occasion to get all equipments ready for their spring farming while all sorts of sales meet people's needs for daily articles.

With the increased level of people's living conditions, supermarkets can be found everywhere in each village. As the transportation develops in countryside, everyone can buy any articles of daily use at any time. Therefore, things on sale in the temple fair are mostly snacks and toys to cater to children. As a result, the function of exchanging things in temple fair diminishes, and the function of entertain ment stands out. The number of passengers flow on Mount Yishan is at its peak on February 2nd, most of them are prayers and visitors for sightseeing. In front of the memorial archway of the

entrance of the mount, opera stages are set up every
year for the opera troupes' performance. According
to local villagers, "February 2nd is the busiest time
for Mount Yishan, as the number of people coming
is even more than that on the New Year's Eve."

山游览的人络绎不绝。
峄山入口处的牌坊前搭
有戏棚，每年的庙会都
会有戏班来唱戏。用当
地村民的话说："每年
二月二是峄山最热闹的
时候，比年三十的人还
要多。"

5

粤南"卖身节"

Festival of Selling Oneself in Southern Guangdong Province

在我国的许多地方，二月二是开耕劳作的日子。过去民间在这一天要进行劳动力交易，并由此形成了很多地方性的节日庆典。广东省东莞市东坑镇二月二卖身节便是一个典型的案例。

一、繁荣的东坑

东坑村又名塘唇村，隶属于广东省东莞市，村中有东坑集市。东坑集市交通方便，水道有神山

In many parts of China, February 2nd is the day people start their farm work. In the past, labor transaction often took place on this day, which led to a variety of local celebrations, for example, the Festival of Selling Oneself at Dongkeng in Dongguan City of Guangdong Province.

1.Prosperous Dongkeng

Dongkeng village is also called Tangchun Village. It is within the boundary of Dongguan City of Guangdong Province. There is a Dongkeng market in the village, where the transportation is

convenient: the waterway goes to Shenshan Dock with ferries to and fro Dongguan, Guangzhou and Huizhou; highways connect Changping, Dalang and Hengli as businessmen from Tangxia, Qingxi, Zhangmutou and Gongming heading for Guangzhou, Shilong and Huizhou all pass through this place. The market of Dongkeng is very prosperous with Leran Street, Zhenxing Street, Yaoxi Street, Qiaotou Street and Baoxing Street and various shops along them. Before the foundation of People's Republic of China, the market of Dongkeng is a large tent of about two hundred square meters behind Leran Street and in front of Zhenxing Street, and it is a market of fish, meat and vegetables, opening in the morning and evening. In the morning, there are fifteen or sixteen booths selling pork and a dozen of booths

码头，客船往返于东莞、广州、惠州之间；陆路有通往常平、大朗、横沥的大道，塘厦、清溪、樟木头、公明等一带的客商必经此地往来于广州、石龙、惠州之间。东坑市场繁荣，乐然街、振兴街、耀西街、桥头街、保兴街一带，店铺林立。新中国成立前，东坑市场设在乐然街后边、振兴街的前边，建有一个约两百平方米的市亭，这就是鱼肉菜市场，早晚开市。早上有十五六档猪肉，十多档鱼货，还有卖牛肉、豆腐，以及卖杂水鱼的、卖蔬菜的，摆满了整个市亭。卖柴地方在石狗村前的乐然街口空地上，大朗一带的人都来这里卖柴。当时东坑外地来客很多，开设有客栈、妓院、赌馆、烟馆等，每年夏秋期间还开设蟀寮（斗蟋蟀的地方），因而有"小澳门"之称。①

二、历史上的卖身节

明清之际，岭南商品经济逐步发展，人口不断增加，同时土地日益集中，农业人口的剩余及转移成为历史的必然。少量的富裕自耕农和佃农开始使用雇工，创造更多的财富，于是，农民破产和沦为雇工的现象成为全国的一个普遍现象。东莞东坑二月二卖身节就是在这种背景下兴起的。

传说明朝万历年间（1573—1620），东坑村有个地主叫卢同锦，要

①东坑镇志办公室：《东坑镇志》,1992年，第38页，内部印刷。

selling fish; the market is also filled with other booths selling beef, bean curd and various fish and vegetables. The opening of the Leran Street in front of Stoned-dog Village is a place where people from Dalang sell firewood. At that time, Dongkeng has many visitors from outside the village, who stay in the inns and go to brothels, gambling houses and opium houses; there are also cricket houses (where people play cricket fighting)in summer and autumn. Therefore, the village is also called "Little Macao". [1]

2.Festival of Selling Oneself in the History

In late Ming Dynasty and early Qing Dynasty, Lingnan commodity economy developed fast as well as the population, while the lands were concentrated day by day into the hands of big landlords, it is an inevitable trend to transfer the surplus rural population. The minority of rich farmers began to hire poor workers to create more wealth, therefore, poor farmers went bankrupted and became employed labors all around the country. This is how the "Festival of Selling Oneself" on February 2nd in Dongkeng and Dongguan came into being.

It is said that in Ming Dynasty under the reign of Wanli (1573—1620), there was a landlord called Lu Tongjin in Dongkeng village who wanted

[1]Dongkeng Town Office: *Records of Dongkeng*,1992, p.38, restricted publication.

to hire a long-time worker for farm work. A lot of other landlords were also in need of labors. Therefore, on February 2nd every year before the spring farming began, large numbers of workers would come to Dongkeng Village looking for an employer to sell their labors. They were wearing bamboo hat on the head and a piece of towel on the shoulder and waited at the crossroad of Dongkeng Village for an employer to make a contract of job and set a favorable price for their labors. Year by year, it becomes a common practice and a labor market comes into being on this very day. This is the beginning of the Festival of Selling Oneself in Dongkeng Village.

As there are a great many people coming from various regions to look for an employer during this period, many retailers also move to this place for business, such as retailers for farming tools and groceries, which becomes the unique market for Dongkeng people. Villagers can buy anything and everything there. It is said that one year during the Festival, a farmer came to the Dongkeng market following its fame but only found that everything was sold out as he was late for the business hour. He said to himself, "I am told that in this market you can buy anything, but now nothing is left for me to buy; if they sell a father, I would buy one." As soon as he finished his complain, there was a voice said, "Yes, we do have a father on sale." The farmer turned back and saw an old man standing there, so he bought him home and treated him as father. Every year, he followed the old man's words to pick up the

雇长工耕作。同村还有不少大户，亦要雇工。故此，每年二月初二开耕之前，都有大批人来东坑找雇主，出卖劳力。他们头戴竹笠，肩搭水布，站在东坑路口等人雇用，价钱面议，当面成交，订立合约，确定雇佣关系。年复一年，袭以成俗，逐渐形成一个劳动力市场。这就是后来的东坑卖身节的由来。

由于各地来此受雇的人很多，小摊贩也应运而生，继之小农具、小百货杂物等摊档也应时而立，形成东坑特有的集市，"什么都有得卖"，"什么东西都可以卖完"。传说有一年卖身节期间，一个慕名而来的农民到东坑应市，来晚了，什么东西都已卖光，他自言自语道："都说东坑什么东西都有得卖，现在什么东西都没得卖，如果有老子卖，我也买一个。"立即有人应声道："有老子卖！"农民回头一看，是一位老人家，即依言将他买回侍奉如亲者子。每年什么时候播种，什么时候插秧，都听老子的。有一年，老子叫那农民晚播种。他就晚播种，别人的稻谷熟了，他的禾身才含胎待吐。正好是那一年，皇帝的龙驹病了，御医说要吃含胎草才能治好，便找到那位农民，买了他的含胎禾苗，治好了龙驹，皇帝大喜，重赏了这位种植含胎草的农民。从此以后，人们去赶东坑集市，不管什么东西，都要买点回去，以示吉祥。真可谓"有老子也买一个回来"。所以卖身节越来越兴旺[①]。

新中国成立后，卖身在建国后土地改革与农业合作化的运动中彻底终结，东坑人不必再去卖身了，卖身节也被改称"翻身节"。但人们依旧怀念往日卖身节上的热闹。"文革"时期，卖身节依然顽强地存在着，

best time for ploughing and seedling. One year, the old man asked him to seed very late, and the son did as he told. When the crops of others riped, his crops were just in their early puberty. Then news came that the Emperor's favorite horse fell ill and the royal doctors believed that only the embryos of plants can save its life. So the farmer was asked to offer his crop embryos and the horse was recovered after eating the offerings. The Emperor was so pleased that he greatly rewarded the farmer. From then on, when people come to the market in Dongkeng, they all buy something home for luck, which is joked as "buy a father home if they have one there in the market", and the Festival becomes more popular in this way.[①]

After 1949, labor selling was ended by the movements of land reform and agriculture cooperation. Villagers in Dongkeng village no longer sell themselves and the "Festival of Selling Oneself" became the "Festival of Freedom". But people still can't forget the liveliness of the old festival day, and during the Culture Revolution period, the Festival

---

①东坑镇志办公室.《东坑镇志》.1992年，第38页，内部印刷。

①Dongkeng Town Office: *Records of Dongkeng*.1992, p.38 restricted publication

was still celebrated as people came to the Dongkeng village from far and near. The festival has a strong vitality with its root among the people. Based on the policy of reforming and opening up, the festival grows into a joyous day for people to visit their families and friends, and exchange the agriculture products. As we enter the 21st century, the day of "selling oneself" has turned into a feature of the local festival celebration with the interference of local authorities, and represents the geographical and cultural tradition of Dongguan, and later the festival becomes the "First Festival" of Dongguan.

3.Customs of "the Festival of Selling Oneself"

a.An Exchange of Labors

According to the proverb, "On February 2nd, when dragon raises its head, the cattle in all families start to work", following the changing of climate, on February 2nd, most parts of our country are influenced by monsoon. As a result, the temperature rise again and the hours of daylight and the rain also increases; there is a favorable condition of light, temperature and water for the growing of crops, especially in countryside in South China. According to the custom of Dongguan, every year the employers decide whether to extend their contracts with the partners on December 16th, and whether to extend their contracts with the long-time workers before the winter solstice day. If the fired workers are given the "heartless chicken" before winter

老百姓仍自发地在四面八方汇集东坑，可见民间节日生命力之顽强。改革开放以后，卖身节逐渐成为人们探亲会友、交换农副产品的佳期。进入21世纪，卖身节在政府的强力介入下俨然成为地方节庆的代表，成为地域传统与文化的表征，更在后来成为远近闻名的"东莞第一节"。

三、卖身节的习俗

（一）劳动力交换

农谚曰："二月二，龙抬头，大家小户使耕牛。"依据气候规律，"二月二"之时，我国大部分地区受季风气候影响，温度回升，日照时数增加，雨水也逐渐增多，光、温、水条件已能满足农作物的生长需要，南方农村更是如此。东莞风俗，每年十二月十六日时决定伙计是否续约；冬至前则决定长工来年续约与否。如果去年冬至节前吃了"无情鸡"，被"炒鱿鱼"的雇农则最迟在二月初二这一天得重新找工作。同样，雇主最迟也需在这天为开耕补充长工。因此，东坑附近的贫民雇工也多在这天上集市"卖身"。

童工交易是民国时期卖身节市场的重要特点，最多的是雇男童做掌牛仔。当时，农户家中的牛足以代表他的殷实和地位。作为最重要的代耕工具，黄牛一个上午可耕地三亩，并可以出租给别人，赚取牛谷；好的耕牛还可以从事蔗糖的压榨生产工作。那时候，娶媳妇要把耕牛牵出来，证明是农耕大户，所以有耕牛的人家都视牛为命根子，要专门找雇童来放养、看护。

各乡贫苦的人家，都带着儿子来这里找寻雇主，而各处的雇主，也就来这里找寻雇童。如果大家讲得合适，那雇童就跟那雇主回家去做工。那些雇童的工作总离不了耕田看牛这几种，除了赚得饭吃之外，完全没有工钱，只是到了年尾的时候，由

solstice festival, they are to find a new job soon before February 2nd. In the same way, employers have to find new workers before the day for the spring farm work. Therefore, poor peasant workers near Dongkeng village often "sell themselves" on this day in the market.

Child laborer transaction was one of the features in the market of labor selling in Republican Period, most of the child laborers were boys to watch over the cows. At that time, the number of cows in a farmer's family represents the financial condition of the household. As an important tool for ploughing, a cow can plough a land of three *mu* (2000 square meters), and it can be rent to others for some income. A good cow can even help in producing sugar from sugarcane. At that time, young men would show the cows of his family to the guests in his wedding to prove that he is a competent farmer. All families with cows saw the security of animals as precious as their own, and they would hire young boys to look after them.

The poor families of the neighboring villages all come with their sons to look for a nice employer, and the employers are looking for a smart cowboy. If both sides manage to reach an agreement, the boy can work for the employer from then on. Their work are no more than working in the fields and looking after the cows, and they have no salary except free meals, and only at the end of the year would the employer give them a set of new clothes and a pair of new shoes as the reward of a year's work. So it is called "selling oneself".[1]

b.Commodity and Trade

In 1920s and 1930s, Dongkeng Village became the hub of land and water transportation in nearby towns, and ferries to and fro Guangzhou, Foshan and Dongguan all take the village as a harbor[2] to rest, as along the river, there are all kinds of shops, including gambling houses, opium houses and brothels. On "Festival of Selling Oneself", besides the traditional exchange of laborers, retailers from all over the rural area would come to Dongkeng market on that day to sell all sorts of toys and snacks as well as other groceries. There are also many entertainment activities such as kongfu performance team, acrobatics performance team of Guangdong and cricket fighting gambling, which attract crowds of people from the neighboring towns.

In 1960s, the festival is cancelled and replaced by the communist educating practice of eating the proletariat meals to recall the dark days and to cherish the life at present, which was organized by each production brigade in Dongkeng Village. Shops were asked to close on that day as their owners had to take part in volunteering work. However, retailers

[1]Li Jianqing. *A Glance of Folk Customs In Dongguan, Folklore.* combined issue 15 and 16, 1928
[2]You can refer to *Transportations of Dongguan.* for descriptions on waterways of Hanxi, compiled by Transportation Bureau of Guangdong, January, 1989, p.31.

雇主给他一套新衣服和一双鞋，就算报酬了，所以叫作"卖身"。[1]

（二）购物商贸

20世纪二三十年代，东坑成为附近城乡水陆运输的枢纽，广州、佛山、东莞等地的渡船往来都以此为埠头[2]，沿河两岸商铺林立，赌馆、烟馆、妓馆歌舞升平。"卖身节"除了约定俗成的劳动力交流之外，各乡的小贩到了那天都办齐很多的玩品和食物以及其他货品，赶到东坑趁市。还有各种功夫武班、粤戏杂耍和蟋蟀赌博等游乐，汇集了附近各镇的成千上万的人流，十分热闹。

到了20世纪60年代，节日庆祝被下令取消。是日，东坑各村每个生产大队要吃"阶级餐"，忆苦思甜，进行共产主义教育；同时勒令商店关门，参加义务劳动。但从各地

[1]李建青：《东莞风俗的一斑》，《民俗》第十五、十六期合刊，1928年。
[2]参见广东省东莞市交通局编：《东莞市交通志》关于寒溪水航道的描述，1989年1月，第31页。

来的摊贩集中在东坑村附近的荔枝园内摆卖，群众一样来趁热闹。由于物质奇缺，许多远道而来的游客，都是吃了早饭而来，许多茶楼饭店也为旅客做好了供应的准备。

1966年"文化大革命"开始后，当时的领导忌讳"卖身"两字，力图"消灭"卖身节，不但不准摆卖商品，还出动真枪实弹的武装民兵，把守路口，驱赶群众。但一到时间，集市依然举行。面对着成千上万的群众，民兵们也无可奈何。由于商品

still gathered in the Litchi Garden near the village to sell their goods, and the market was always filled with buyers on that day. At that time, people were almost short of everything, from food to clothes, so many visitors coming all the way to the market set out early after breakfast, and the restaurants in the market also prepared delicious dinners for them.

When Cultural Revolution began in 1966, the authorities did not like the words "Selling Oneself", so they made every effort to "wipe out" the festival. Retailing booths were not allowed and militiamen with arms were asked to guard every crossroad to drive away the buyers. But when the day arrived, the market was held as always. And militiamen could do nothing about millions of buyers. Due to the shortage of commodities at that time, the market played a role of adjustment and supplement to people's life. In this special period of political movements, the festival was suspended only once or twice.

At the end of 1970s, the festival was revived among people. Due to the desire to exchange the goods and the cohesive force of the traditional festival, more and more people came back to the market in front of the Lu's Ancestral Hall in Dongkeng village for trading and visiting their relatives and friends.

From 1980s to 1990s, the festival was maintained and developed by people's enthusiasm. Old-fashioned farming tools and groceries were still on sale in the remains of the market, and there were traditional toys[1] such as hand-made kylin's head, lion's head and figurines of Big Head Buddha, which are rarely seen in town today. The visitors often brought one or two home for fun.

c. Visiting Relatives and Friends

The Festival of Selling Oneself provides an occasion for the employers and workers to make contracts with each other, and it's also for families

---

[1] They are made from thick paper or newspaper with bamboo branches by hand; they are hollow in the middle and have beautiful colors painted on the surface. If waving them on the head, they look extremely fantastic and fun.

奇缺，卖身节市场起到一定的弥补与调节作用。卖身节在那段非常的政治运动时期，实际上也就中断过一两次而已。

20世纪70年代末，卖身节在民间复苏。出于对物质交流的渴望以及节庆信仰的凝聚力，人们越来越多地回到东坑村卢氏祠堂前进行商品交易、探亲访友等。

20世纪80年代至90年代，卖身节被民间力量自发地维系与发展。集市上继续摆卖着旧式农具和传统日用品、工艺品，还有供小孩子玩的小麒麟头、狮子头、大头佛等传统玩具出售。[1]如今城里的孩子已极少能见到这些传统玩具了，前来游玩的人也乐于图个新鲜，买上一两件回家。

（三）走亲访友

卖身节是劳动力雇佣双方交易的集中市场，还是亲朋好友团聚的"旺

---

[1] 这些东西都是手工制作的，用厚纸皮或报纸，加上竹枝做成，中间空，用来举戴在头上舞动，表面上涂上了鲜艳的色彩，好看又好玩。

日"。东坑人在卖身节期间有个习俗，全家要团聚在一起吃饭。届时，亲朋好友也会过来串门吃饭，人们把这一天的交往也看成一种会带来吉祥的行为。朋友往往会带他的朋友来，却不需要提前打招呼，只需告诉主人家有几个人来吃，便可到集市上购物，中午再回来吃饭。期间，主人家会按人数准备饭菜招呼客人。吃过饭，亲戚往往便会散去。亲戚朋友多的，家里往往需晚上再开几桌。这天谁家客人多，谁家脸上便有光。

and friends to get together. Dongkeng Villagers have a festival practice of the family members sitting around the table to have a dinner together when all the relatives come to the house, which is considered as an auspicious reunion. Friends would bring more friends to the dinner without calling in advance, but the host should be informed of the number of guests before the dinner so that he could buy enough cooking materials in the market. The guests come at noon and the dishes are already placed on the table for them according to the number of people. The relatives would leave soon after the dinner. If it is an extended family with large numbers of relatives and friends, several more tables will be presented for the guests to sit around. The more guests, the more proud the host is.

Dinners in festival provide an opportunity for relatives and friends to know each other better. Villagers are pleased to see groups of relatives and friends coming to their house; they never consider it as a troublesome matter, but believe that more guests will bring more liveliness to the house, which is a sign of prosperity and happiness. The desire for good luck and a close connection of kinship and friendship makes the practice of visiting relatives and friends an important custom in the festival.

d. The Game of Water Shooting

One of the eye-catching activities in the festival is the game of water shooting, which is a newly invented "tradition" with a history of dozens of years.

The game of water shooting was unexpectedly welcomed by people, especially young people, since its first appearance in the market. More and more young people take part in the game and water shooting in Dongkeng market becomes the main celebration of the festival for them. The game brings a cheerful and exciting experience to the participants, who not only bring the new tools for water shooting but also promote the game's development. Attention from media also help in the development of the game, as water shooting becomes the symbol of the festival in their reports.

节日里的聚餐，毫无疑问为亲戚朋友提供了一次交往的机会。村民们乐意看到一批批亲戚朋友前来串门吃饭，他们不认为这是件麻烦的事情，相反认为更多的朋友能带来更多的人气，而人气有时候就是兴旺、吉祥的好兆头。这种求吉的心理和对亲情、友情交往的渴望，使得卖身节期间的走亲访友成为一种重要的节俗。

（四）射水狂欢

卖身节期间如今最吸引眼球的活动无疑是射水狂欢。它是节庆中新近发明的一项"传统"，至今仅有十余年的历史。

射水活动出现之后，意外地得到了民众们的积极参与，尤其是年轻人。越来越多的年轻人在这一天把去东坑射水作为卖身节过节的主要方式。当越来越多的人发现射水能带来愉悦和刺激时，他们便带来更为新式的射水枪械，更推动了射水活动的大规模发展。其中，媒体的相关报道也开始推波助澜，把射水当成卖身节的

代名词。有些媒体甚至将其与傣族的泼水节相联系，这种影响后来一直延续，并通过政府介入而正式被认可，并成为卖身节活动的重要环节。

四、结语

东坑二月二卖身节由最初的劳动力交易市场演化而来，在上百年的历史发展中，与当地的集市贸易相融合，并不断增添新

Some of the journalists even associate it with the Water-Sprinkling Festival of Dai people. The influence of the game never fades away, and with the acknowledgement of the authorities, the practice of water shooting becomes an essential part of the festival activities.

4.Conclusion

The Festival of Selling Oneself on February 2nd in Dongkeng village is transformed from the labor trade and integrated into the local trading activities in its development of hundreds of years. It breathes a new life to the festival customs and creates the unique festival activities in local area. The government plays an active role in encouraging the development of the festival. It shows that the Festival of Selling Oneself adjusts itself to the change of the society, to cater to the needs of people in modern time, and finally becomes the "Number One Festival" in Dongguan. This is where the strong vitality of folk festival lies.

的节俗内容，成为一个颇具地域特色的节庆活动。其中，政府的积极引导扮演着重要的角色。可以说，卖身节的节庆活动不断被政府整合。我们从中看到的是，东坑卖身节随着社会的变迁，不断调整自己前进的步伐，去满足民众的需求，并最终成为东莞市的"第一节"。这正是民间传统节日强大的生命力所在。

6

粤西南"梁镇南将军府炮会"

Cannon Ceremony in the Mansion of General Liang Zhennan in Southwest of Guangdong

The tradition of holding a cannon ceremony is observed in many places of Guangdong Province. Cannon ceremony is also called "grabbing for firecrackers","grabbing for firecracker flower" and "the day of firecrackers". It started in late Ming

广东省许多地区有在过年过节期间举行炮会的传统。炮会，也被称作"抢炮头""抢炮花""炮期"等，大约起源于明末清初，举办时间多集中在正月十六和二月初二期间，主要内容为燃烧特制的鞭炮，并抢夺其燃放升空后掉下来的、具有良好寓意的"炮圈"。一些地方的"炮会"在新中国成立后曾消逝，而在近十多年开始慢慢恢复。广东省阳春市石望镇交岗村的"梁镇南将军府炮会"就是一个颇有地域特色的盛会。

一、炮会起源

石望镇交岗村地处云雾山脉下段、漠阳江上游，村中鱼塘众多，塘中野藕不种自生，风景十分宜人。相传，该村的"梁镇南将军府炮会"起源于明朝弘治年间（1488—1505），为纪念本村梁姓子孙梁镇南将军而设立。梁镇南自小好武，练得一身好本领，尤其是臂力过人，有运斤成风的本领。明朝时期，两广的瑶民起义不断，历时一百多年，动乱之策源地在广西浔州（今桂平）大藤峡。明成

Dynasty and early Qing Dynasty, and was held on January 16th and February 2nd of the lunar year. The firecrackers made for this occasion are burnt and the ash of them are caught by people as a sign of good will. The cannon ceremony in some places faded away after 1949, but is reviving in recent dozens of years. The cannon ceremony in the Mansion of General Liang Zhennan in Jiaogang Village, Shiwang County of Yangchun City, Guangdong Province is a grand occasion in local area.

1. The Origin of Cannon Ceremony

Jiaogang Village of Shiwang County is seated at the lower part of the Mountain Cloud, and the upper stream of Moyang River. There are many fishponds with naturally grown lotus in them. It is a place with beautiful scenery. It is said that the cannon ceremony in this village can be traced back to the Reign of Hongzhi, Ming Dynasty (1488—1505), in memory of Liang Zhennan, a son of the Liang family in the village who was conferred the title of General at that time. Liang Zhennan was fond of kongfu at an early age and was trained with fighting skills. He also had a pair of strong arms, which could easily lift any heavy burdens. In Ming Dynasty, the Yao people in Guangdong and Guangxi staged a uprising lasting over a hundred years, the center of which was in Dateng Gorge of Xunzhou(the ancient name of

Guiping), Guangxi. In 1465, Liang Zhennan went to the gorge with the army of 160,000 soldiers, led by Han Yong, the vice minister of Military Department and Officer of Guangdong, to fight against the rebelling army. In the war, Liang Zhennan showed his wisdom as well as courage, and won so many battles that he was given the title "General Tiger". To honor his achievements, the imperial court gave him a mansion named "the House of General Liang Zhennan". On the day he returned to his hometown, the whole village came out to welcome him.

化元年（1465年），梁镇南随兵部侍郎、广东按察使韩雍率领的十六万大军进入广西浔州大藤峡，征剿乱匪。在战争中，梁镇南智勇双全，屡立战功，官至"二品顶戴殿前虎贲将军"。为表彰其功勋，朝廷在他告老还乡之时，在其家乡建造"梁镇南将军府。梁镇南返乡当天，

全村男女老少外出迎接，夹道欢迎。村中自发用五个炮筒装好火药，连放五发。此后，每年二月初二都会聚会鸣炮，来颂扬梁将军忠义为国的非凡功绩，这就是后来的梁镇南将军府炮会。

二、炮会现场

二月初一当天，交岗村的村道已经插满了彩旗，村里停放有许多外地牌照的车辆，据介绍是外出居住或工作的村民专程返乡参加次日举行的炮会。炮会的一个重要场所——梁镇南将军府兼梁氏宗祠，已经开始聚集了许多乡亲。炮会理事会成员在那里商议炮会的事宜，还有从外面聘请过来的醒狮队在做表演前的准备。夜幕降临，将军府内响起了锣鼓声，醒狮表演开始了。村民们围坐在四周，一边聊天，一边观看表演。整场表演持续到晚上十一点才散场。在二月初一这天，每家都会包粽子、做油酪，准备次日的肉食。

Villagers set up five cannons with gun powders in it and fired five shells in a row. After that, every year on February 2nd, the villagers would get together to set off the firecrackers and cannons in memory of the achievements of General Liang, and later it became the practice of cannon ceremony we know today.

2. The Site of Cannon Ceremony

On the first day of February, the road is lined with colorful flags and many vehicles hanging non-local licence plates, the owners of which are villagers working and living outside and returning to the village for the celebration the next day. One of the important site, the Ancestral Temple of Liang Family and the Mansion of General Liang Zhennan is already crowded with many villagers. Members of the celebration council are discussing the arrangement of this year's ceremony, and a lion dancing team hired from outside the village is making their last minute preparation before the performance. When the night falls, the sound of gongs and drums is heard from the General's mansion, announcing the beginning of the lion dancing performance. Villagers sit around the stage, talking while enjoying the performance, which lasts until eleven o'clock at night. On February 1st, all households would make *Zongzi* (traditional Chinese rice-pudding), fried cakes and meat for the next day.

On the morning of February 2nd, women of the village are busy cooking in the kitchen of the mansion of the General. Council members wearing the flower-made balls greet the guests coming all the way from Enping City and Yangjiang City of Jiangmen, Guangdong. The most respectable guests are wearing a flower-decorated card with "VIP" on it.

When midday is approaching, a roasted pig is carried into the mansion and the host starts to worship the gods with all of the representatives of the guests. They are worshipping General Liang Zhennan and the ancestors of Liang Family. During this ritual, villagers all offer the sacrifice of their

二月初二一早，将军府后堂的厨房里，村里的妇女在热火朝天地张罗着饭菜。炮会理事会的成员则胸前佩戴着理事会的花球，迎接陆续从广东江门恩平市、阳江市等地前来的宗亲和宾客；一些重要的客人还会别上"贵宾"的胸花。

临近中午，一只烧猪被抬进将军府内，主事组织代表拜神。所拜的是梁镇南将军和梁氏历代祖先。期间，各家的村民也陆续带着自家的祭品（鸡、鸭等）前来拜祭。待拜过神后，各家派出一名代表，和外地来的宾客一起在将军府内共进午餐。

下午3点，炮会即将举行。醒狮队在将军府内举行一阵表演式的叩拜礼仪后，五位事先选定的小孩分别捧着1~5号大炮依次站在前面，后面紧跟着人扛着大饼状的鞭炮（十万头、二十万头规格）的村民，再接着是旗手、醒狮队和其他村民。一阵鞭炮响过，队伍向着村后距将军府约5分钟路程的炮场出发。

炮场，也就是集中燃放大炮和成捆鞭炮的空地。这里在二月初一当天已经搭建起一个主席台，上面挂着"交岗梁镇南将军府炮会"的横幅。待村民到齐后，主事会先行到土地公烧香拜祭后才由会长宣布炮会开始。先燃放的是小礼炮，共5发。接着点燃5发大炮，这5发"炮"也有名称：一炮名"万紫千红"；二炮名"花开富贵"；

own house (chicken and ducks) to worship. After that, each family sends a representative to have lunch with the guests from outside the village in General's Mansion.

At three o'clock in the afternoon, the cannon ceremony begins. Firstly, the lion dancing team gives a performance of kowtowing and worshipping inside the mansion; then five chosen children carry the cannon No. 1 to No.5 and stand in a line, followed by people carrying huge, round firecrackers (about one hundred thousand to two hundred thousand heads in each firecrackers) and flag bearers as well as the lion dancing team and the villagers. In the sound of firecrackers, the group march towards the cannon field which is five minutes' walk from General's Mansion.

The cannon field is where the cannons and firecrackers are set off together. On February 1st, an auditorium has been set up there with a banner of "Cannon Ceremony of Mansion of General Liang Zhennan in Jiaogang Village" hanging up over the stage. When the auditorium is filled with villagers, the host will worship the God of Earth with some burning incenses and the head of the council gives the official announcement of the opening of the cannon ceremony. Firstly, five firecrackers are set off. Then the five cannons are lighted. Each of the five cannons has got a name of its own: No. 1 is called "colorfulness"; No.2 is called "wealth blossoming like flowers"; No.

3 is called "more money and more sons"; No.4 is called "luck and fortune filled in the house"; No.5 is called "happiness and longevity". The cannons are lighted in the order of their numbers. Two "lions" will dance around each cannon for several rounds before it is set off, and ordinary firecrackers are set off when they are dancing. The five cannons are lighted by the most respectable persons in the village, mostly the officials of the village or the person who donated the largest amount of money for the council.

When the sound of the cannon flying to the sky is heard, villagers all swarm forward to try to get the "cannon circle". The one who gets it is called "the head of the cannon". The fiercest competition for "cannon circle" is the fight for No.3, the cannon of "more money and more sons". The heads of the cannon are coming home with their prizes, surrounded by lion dancing team and the sound of drums and gongs. When they return home, they will hang up the cannon circles in the middle of their sitting room. On the evening of February 2nd, a

三炮名"添丁发财";四炮名"满堂吉庆";五炮名"福寿双辉"。按照炮号从1~5依次燃放,每燃放一枚大炮时,都先由两头"狮子"绕着那枚大炮舞数圈,期间燃放普通鞭炮。5发大炮均由村里德高望重的人点燃,一般是官员或者是向炮会捐款较多者。

每一发大炮响起,围观的村民就一哄而上,争抢"炮圈"。抢得"炮圈"者被称为"炮首",其中以寓意"添丁发财"的三炮抢夺最为激烈。"炮首"会在狮子队的簇拥下,一路敲锣打鼓回到家中,将"炮圈"悬挂在家中大堂的中央。二月初二的晚上,炮会理事会组

织村民在将军府前的空地上燃放烟花，村民隔着一口鱼塘观看焰火。

农历二月初三，是每年炮会的最后一天。这天，各家会派出一名代表到将军府开会。内容是总结本届炮会情况，商议明年炮会的计划，同时公布本届炮会的账目。会议进行至上午11点半左右结束，然后是午饭时间。在饭桌上，村民会许愿，就是把自己的愿望说出来，让同桌的人听到。有的

firework performance is arranged by the council of cannon ceremony in the open in front of the mansion and the villagers are able to enjoy it at the other end of the fishpond.

On February 3rd, the last day of cannon ceremony, every family send a representative to the Mansion of the General for a meeting of concluding the ceremony of this year and planning for the next year's celebration activities. The accounts and expenditure of this year's celebration are made public on this meeting, which ends at about half past eleven and is followed by the lunch. At dinner table, villagers would make wishes that are loud enough to be heard by other members of the table. Some would say, "If I have a son next year, I will donate 1000 yuan to the council." Most of the wishes are concerned with having more sons.

3.Conclusion

"Cannon Ceremony of the Mansion of General Liang Zhennan" in Jiaogang village of Shiwang Town, Yangchun City, Guangdong Province has such a long history and is still popular in these days, thanks to the entertament elements of the "head of cannon competition" so that everyone can take

人会说："如果我明年生了个儿子，我就向炮会捐1000元。"而大多数村民的愿望就是添丁。

三、结语

广东阳春石望镇交岗村"梁镇南将军府炮会"流传至今而不衰，在很大程度上是因为其"抢炮头"环节的娱乐性、狂欢性和广泛参与性。尽管抢得"炮圈"成为"炮首"者有"万紫千红"、"花开富贵""添丁发财""满堂吉庆"和"福寿双辉"五个不同层次的寓意，但作者在当地听闻最多的是关于"添丁"的议论。毕竟，"万紫千红""满堂吉庆"等形容词过于虚渺，不容易鉴别是否灵验，而"添丁"是实实在在的。这也在某种程度上折射出了"重男轻女"思想在当地农村的根深蒂固，这种情感的纠结，或许正是"炮会"节俗流传不衰的原动力。

part in it and enjoy it. Those who get the "cannon circle" and become the head of cannons will be blessed with various auspicious significances of the cannons, such as "colorful life", "wealth blossoming like flowers", "more money and more sons", "luck and fortune filled in the house" and "happiness and longevity", but most people would like to be blessed with "more sons", as blessings like "colorful life" and "luck and fortune" are too idealistic to realize, but "more sons" is realistic and needed by most families. It reflects to some extent that the thought of "boys being better than girls" is deeply rooted in rural areas. This complicated emotion might be the motivation of making people's minds in the "cannon ceremony" enjoy such a time-honored popularity among villagers.

坐在将军府大院，观看醒狮舞动，听锣鼓喧天爆竹声声，当年梁镇南将军征战沙场的英姿豪气犹在眼前。人们一年一度地举行"梁镇南将军府炮会"，其目的就在于纪念先人丰功伟绩，启迪后人奋发上进吧。

When you sit in the courtyard of the Mansion of the General, watching the dancing lions and listening to the sound of drums, gongs and firecrackers, the bright and valiant look of General Liang in the battlefield will be incarnuted in front of you. The purpose for people to hold the "cannon ceremony" in the Mansion of General Liang is to commemorate the achievements of their ancestors and inspire the young people to work hard and do better.

When the Festival
of February 2nd Is Fading away

余论：渐行渐远的
二月二

Influenced by the trend of modernization and globalization, Chinese society in its transitional period is experiencing the rapid transformation from a traditional agricultural society lasting for thousands of years to the modern industrial society. At the same time, with the fast development of information industry, modern information technology brings benefits to the public; conventional concepts of time and space and ways of communicating take on a new look. The rhythms of people's life also change greatly with new needs coming up. Against this background, traditional festivals closely related to the old farming culture lose their soil of survival. Festivals that take their shape in agriculture society, such as the Festival of February 2nd, are hard to connect themselves to the modern society, which accounts for its decline today. Like other traditional festivals, the Festival of February 2nd is in a disadvantaged position in the modern trend where time is well-divided, the pace of life is faster, and the line between offering service and receiving service is well-defined.

在现代化、全球化的影响下，中国社会目前处于转型期，正在经历着从已持续数千年的传统农业社会向现代工业社会的急剧转变。同时，伴随着信息产业的飞速发展，现代信息技术逐渐惠及普通民众，传统的时空观念和交流方式发生了巨大变化。民众的生活节律由此发生了巨大的改变，并产生了种种新的需求。以此为背景，与传统农耕文明关系密切的传统节日失去了原有的生存土壤。像二月二这种在农耕社会中定型、成熟的节日，很难与现代社会相对接，这是它在今天走向衰弱的主要原因。它和一些传统节日一样，在讲究时间分割、节奏快捷、提供服务和接受服务界限分明的现代化潮流中已然处于绝对劣势。伴随现代化的发展，人对大自然的依赖感降低了，对大自然的敏感度也同样降低了。人的生活方式发生了改变，许多地区的农民不再单纯地依附土地，而是长年在外打工或者每天有规律地上下班工作，这就打破了在传统农耕社会中形成的作息时间体系。迫于紧张的生活节奏，许多村民在遵从传统习俗时已是力不从心。于是，二月二炒料豆的人家越来越少，大街小巷处处遥闻炒豆声的昔日场景早已风光不再，撒灰、打囤等也只是老年人的专利，而领龙、驱虫、祀土地、占岁、佩戴龙尾等多已不见，相关禁忌也鲜见遵奉。二月二的衰微，在所难免。

然而，这不等于说二月二在现代社会就失去了存在的价值和意义。二月二毕竟是一个历史悠久的传统节日，经过千百年的沉淀，它早已成为民

People's dependence on the nature is dropping with the rise of modernization, so does their sensitiveness towards the nature. They changed their way of living as farmers in many regions no longer rely on the land to make a living, but work in the urban area in regular hours all year round. Many villagers feel reluctant to observe the traditional customs due to the intense the pace of life. Therefore, fewer and fewer families make fried beans on February 2nd, and the familiar sound of frying beans in every street disappears. Ash-spreading and drawing granaries are only maintained among the old people. The festival practice of leading the dragons, expelling insects, worshipping the earth, making divination for the coming year and wearing "dragon tails" are all hardly seen, and related taboos are rarely observed. The future of the festival is doomed to decline.

However, it does not mean that February 2nd has lost its value of existence and significance. The Festival of February 2nd is a time-honored traditional festival, and has already been a symbol of national life and the carrier of historical memory accumulated for thousands of years. Its festival activities have special functions in modern China: it strengthens a living memory of history and the national self-identity in emotion; it adjusts the relationship between mankind and nature and among people themselves; it brings good mood to individuals. In a world, where modernization, globalization and urbanization become the trends of development, a deep communication among people is more desired than anything else, as people look forward to a close and harmonious relationship with the nature to achieve "returning to nature" in its real sense. Traditional festivals are of special significance in this perspective. Perhaps we do not like to follow all of the festival customs of February 2nd, but the national memory and sentiment embraced on this day is flowing in the blood of every Chinese and becomes a collective consciousness, or rather collective unconsciousness of a nation. The aged often talk about February 2nd as they recollect the good old days and rethink about their life experiences from the depth of their memory, which can be recognized as a determined return to the spiritual homeland of one's own nation.

We found out in our field that the Festival of February 2nd is making every effort with its strong vitality to fit into the needs of modern society. New festival customs are springing up with great

族生活的象征、历史记忆的载体，其节俗活动在今天仍然具有特殊的功能，如强化历史记忆和民族情感认同，调剂人与自然、人与人之间的关系，调整个体身心状态等。越是现代化、全球化、都市化，人们其实越渴望人与人之间的深度沟通，渴望在人与大自然密切交流、和谐相处意义上的"返本还源"。正是在这一点上，传统节日有特别重要的意义。也许，很多二月二节俗活动我们未必愿意遵从，但关于二月二的民族记忆和民族感情，千百年来已经渗入每一个中国人的血液，成为一种民族的集体意识或集体无意识。很多上了年纪的人都对二月二津津乐道，这不仅仅是出于一种怀旧心理，也是在记忆重温中对自身人生阅历的意义追认，和对自己所处民族国家精神家园的矢志回归。

我们在田野调查中发现，二月二正以其顽强的生命力去适应现代社会的种种需求，许多新的节俗悄然兴起，且具有很强的吸引力，从而使得二月二在某些地区重新焕发出节日的活力。如在广东省东莞市东坑镇，二月二已由传统的卖身节演变为民众的狂欢节和购物节，成为当地的"文化名片"。在山东，二月二期间有许多庙会活动，其中的娱乐与物质交易的成分逐步增多，在调节当地民众生活和推动地方经济增长方面发挥着重要作用，因而受到官方和民众普遍重视。所有这些都表明，二月二在现代社会中处于适应与重构的过程，这个过程离不开官方有意识的重构与引导、学者的研究、媒体的宣传和民众的传承再造。

传统节日就像京剧、太极拳、国画等一样，散发着一种醇酽悠长的传统韵味。当一个人从一味的社会纷争中蓦然回首，淡泊名利，又有谁不愿意将自己的文化生命与一个伟大民族的文化传统拥抱呢？就此而言，节日代表了民族国家内在的文化力

attractions, making the festival glow in a joyful vigor in many places and regions. For example, in Dongkeng Town, Dongguan City of Guangdong Province, February 2nd has been transformed from traditional Festival of Selling Oneself to the carnival and shopping festival for all, and it becomes the symbol of local culture. In Shandong, many temple fair activities are held during the festival; most of the activities are related to entertainments and trades, which play an important role in improving people's life and promoting local economic growth; as a result, they are highly recognized by authorities as well as the public. It is indicated that the Festival of February 2nd is involved in a process of readjusting and rebuilding, which relies on the conscious guiding and reconstructing of the authorities, the researches of the scholar, the broadcasting of the media and people's willingness to carry it on.

Traditional festivals send out a mellow smell of tradition, like Peking Opera, Tai Chi (a kind of traditional Chinese shadow boxing) and Chinese paintings. When we look back from the mundane world, we would not think much of fame and gain any more, but embrace the cultural tradition of a great nation with his own cultural life. Who will refuse it? In terms of this philosophy, festivals represent the inner cultural force of a nation and a country, and they embody the cultural identity.

From cultural connotation to cultural memory and cultural symbol, the three elements form the root, the stem and the leaf of the tree of traditional festivals, which nourish and represent the deep soil of Chinese culture. It seems to be a reverse towards the modernization drive, but in the real sense, staying close to the traditional festivals is of great significance, where people find themselves to be "an integral part of nature" and keep a healthy body and mind. Traditional festivals signify the way of living we are looking for and building, which refers to "living in a poetic manner". Here, I would like to appeal to everyone: please pay more attention to our shared festivals and be the carriers of the festival culture. Be part of it and bring forth new ideas in this culture relay to make our festival culture glow in fresh vitality.

量，是文化身份的体现。可以说，从文化内涵到文化记忆、文化符号，三者形成了传统节日之树的根茎叶，众多节日滋养、表征着中华民族的文化厚土。看似相对于现代化运动的逆向而动，其实贴近传统节日是具有重新寻找"天人合一"境界、找回身心健康的深刻意义的。传统节日是我们寻找、建构"诗意地栖居"的生活方式时不可凌越的象征符号。在此，我愿向大家呼吁，关注我们共同的节日，自觉担当节日文化传承的主人，亲力亲为，在传承中创新，让我们的节日文化重新焕发出生机活力吧。

后 记

后 记

　　奉献于诸君面前的这本小书，所以能在短短一个月内脱稿，与包括两位作者在内的"二月二"项目组在近五年来持续的田野研究是分不开的。这是我必须首先说明的。

　　2008年2月，我接受文化部民族民间文艺发展中心委托，承担了国家财政部经费资助项目"中国节日志"（李松主持；该项目又在2010年被批准为国家社科基金特别委托项目）中的第一批试点项目"二月二"。在设计该项目操作框架的过程中，两位老友耿波博士、张勃博士鼎力相助，每每使我有顿开茅塞之感。尤其是张勃，慨然承担起关于"二月二"项目的"综述"和"志略"部分，使我得以集中精力专务调查报告部分的田野点选择、调查团

Postscript

The book presented in front of you is accomplished in one month's time. Thanks to the four years of continuous fieldwork by the *Festival of February 2nd* project team, including the two co-authors. This is what I want to tell you in the first place.

In February, 2008, I was appointed by National and Folk Arts Development Center of Ministry of Culture to write this book *Festival of February 2nd*, which is among the first pilot projects of the Ministry-of- Finance-sponsored project *Chinese Festivals* (directed by Li Song and approved as Special Project funded by National Social and Science Foundation in 2010). Dr. Geng Bo and Dr. Zhang Bo, two of my old friends helped me and inspired me with excellent ideas in my designing of the working frame for the project. Zhang took up the task of writing the "summary" and "introduction" parts of the project, so that I could concentrate on the tasks of selecting the fieldwork sites for survey reports, organizing the research team and coordinating the working schedule. Generally speaking, I chose 14 places in 9 provinces and regions across the Yangtze River

178

for fieldwork researches, which led to a fruitful result containing 350,000 words and over 3,000 pictures, as well as large numbers of recordings and videotapes. In particular, the 9 research teams formed for the project have finished 14 research reports after hard fieldwork, which contain almost all the festival customs of February 2nd and reflect the festival features of February in mainland China in a comprehensive manner and inner connections of regional social life represented by the 14 research sites. The rich first-hand material provides a firm support of facts from daily life for my writing this book. Here, I would like to mention the names of the head of each research team, they are: Ji Guoxiu (Liaoning Province), Xu Tianji (Beijing), Wang Junxia (Hebei Province), Qi Xiaoping (Gansu Province), Zhang Shishan (Shandong Province), Ma Guangting (Jiangsu Province), Qiu Guozhen (Zhejiang Province), Lü Hongyan (Guangxi Province) and Yan Jiang (Guangdong Province). We become friends as we work for this project. In addition, the "summary" and "introduction" parts written by Zhang Bo also contribute to this project. Here I'd like to send my gratitude to all of them.

队组建和工作进度的协调推进。大致说来，该项目共选择田野调查点14个，跨越大江南北9省区，最终形成35万字、图片3000多幅的结项成果，获得为数不菲的录音、录像资料。特别值得一提的是，为完成该项目而组建的9个调查小组，经过辛苦的田野作业，撰写调查报告14个，基本囊括了我国二月二期间的主要节俗事象，全面反映了我国大陆地区二月二的节日生态以及与各调查点所代表的区域社会生活的内在联系。这些丰富的第一手资料，为本书的撰写提供了坚实的生活支撑。在此，应该提及各组负责人的名字，他们是吉国秀（辽宁）、徐天基（北京）、王均霞（河北）、戚晓萍（甘肃）、张士闪（山东）、马光亭（江苏）、邱国珍（浙江）、吕红艳（广西）、阎江（广东）。在完成该项目的过程中，我们也结下了深厚的情谊。在撰写该书的过程中，张勃为该项目撰写的"综述"和"志略"这两部分成果尤其使我们获益良多。感谢他们!

感谢这套丛书的主编李松和副主编张刚!他们为我提供了进入二月二这一研究领域的契机,而这也成为我们之间在节日研究方面持续合作的良好开端。2009年,文化部民族民间文艺发展中心在山东大学设立"中国节日文化研究基地",委托我所在的民俗学研究所承担了《春节山东卷》《七月半》等一批节日志课题,为有着悠久传统的山东大学民俗学学科发展注入了新的活力;2010年,该中心与山东大学合作、委托民俗学研究所编辑出版的《节日研究》(李松、张士闪主编)问世,至今已经推出6辑,获得了较好的学术影响。这期间,我陆续参加了国务院参事室、中央文史馆组织的与节日文化有关的多项活动,如2010年2月的首届春节文化论坛、2011年2月的"春节文化的传承与创新"课题调研组、6

I am also grateful to Li Song, the chief editor and Zhang Gang, the associate editor of this series of books. They offered me an opportunity to enter the domain of studying the Festival of February 2nd. In 2009, Chinese Festival Culture Research Base was established in Shandong University by National and Folk Arts Development Center of Ministry of Culture, and the Folklore Research Institute where I worked was in charge of a number of festival records research programs such as *Spring Festival in Shandong and In the Middle of July*, which breathe a new life into the subject development of folklore in *Shandong University. In 2010, the book Festival Research* (edited by Li Song and Zhang Shishan) was published, which was co-sponsored by the Center and Shandong University and compiled by the Folklore Research Institute. Now the fifth volume of this series of books has just come out and has achieved a positive academic influence. During this period, I have taken part in a variety of activities related to festival culture organized by the Counselor Office of the State Council and Research Institute of Culture and History, including the First Forum on Spring Festival Culture in February, 2010, the research team on "Inheritance and Innovation of Spring Festival Culture" in February, 2011 and its symposium in June as well as the Second Forum on Spring Festival Culture in November. I have published a number of theses on festival researches

on *Guangming Daily, Henan Social Sciences, Shandong Social Sciences* and *Festival Studies,* and started the "February 2nd" Talk Column in *Beijing Daily* and *Qilu Evening Paper.* I have made a full use of the four years' time closely observe and study the Festival of February 2nd, a typical agricultural festival, and finally, get a better and deeper understanding of the time schedule as well as the cultural system of Chinese traditional festivals.

Last but not least, I am grateful to Ms Liu Xi of The National Festival Committee of CUAES, and editors from Anhui People's Publishing House. The book cannot be published in such a short time without their elaborate efforts.

Zhang Shishan
June 3th, 2013

月的"春节文化的传承与创新"座谈会、11月的第二届春节文化论坛等，在《光明日报》《河南社会科学》《山东社会科学》《节日研究》等发表节日研究系列论文，并在《北京日报》《齐鲁晚报》等作专版的"二月二"访谈。五年的时间不长也不短，我通过对"二月二"这一典型农事节日的悉心观察与静心玩味，对我国传统节日的时间制度与文化体系有了较深入的感悟和理解。

最后，还要感谢中国民族节庆专业委员会的刘茜女士，安徽人民出版社的编辑人员，没有他们的精心运作，该书在如此之短的时间内出版是不可能的。

张士闪
2013年6月3日

《中国节庆文化》丛书后记

The Postscript of
Chinese Festival Culture Series

上下五千年的悠久历史孕育了灿烂辉煌的中华文化。中国地域辽阔，民族众多，节庆活动丰富多彩，而如此众多的节庆活动就是一座座珍贵丰富的旅游资源宝藏。在中华民族漫长的历史中所形成的春节、清明、端午、中秋、重阳等众多传统节日和少数民族节日，是中华民族优秀传统文化的历史积淀，是中华民族精神和情感传承的重要载体，是维系祖国统一、民族团结、文化认同、社会和谐的精神纽带，是中华民族生生不息的不竭动力。

为了传播中华民族优秀传统文化，打造中国的优秀民族节庆品牌，中国人类学民族学研究会民族节庆专业委员会与安徽人民出版社合作，在

China has developed its splendid and profound culture during its long history of 5000 years. It has a vast territory, numerous ethnic groups as well as the colorful festivals. The rich festival activities have become the invaluable tourism resources. The traditional festivals, such as the Spring Festival, the Tomb-Sweeping Day, the Dragon Boat Festival, the Mid-Autumn Day and the Double-Ninth Festival as well as the festivals of ethnic minorities, are representing the excellent traditional culture of China and have become an important carrier bearing the spirits and emotions of the Chinese people, the spirit bond of the national reunification, national unity, cultural identity and social harmony, and an inexhaustible driving force for the development of the Chinese Nation.

In order to spread the excellent traditional culture of China and build the folk festival brand for our country, the Folk Festival Commission of the China Union of Anthropological and Ethnological Science (CUAES) has worked with the Anhui People's Publishing House to publish the *Chinese*

Festival Culture Series under the support from the State Council Information Office. For this purpose, the Folk Festival Commission has established the editorial board of the *Chinese Festival Culture Series*, by inviting Mr. Steven Wood Schmader, the president and CEO of the International Festival and Events Association (IFEA); Mr. Feng Jicai, the executive vice-president of China Federation of Literary and Art Circles; Mr. Zhou Mingfu, the vice-chairman of the China Union of Anthropological and Ethnological Science (CUAES); Mr. Huang Zhongcai, the deputy director of the politics research office of the National Ethnic Affairs Commission, and the secretary-general of the China Union of Anthropological and Ethnological Science (CUAES); Ms. Wu Cuiying , the director of the Cultural Promotion Department of the National Ethnic Affairs Commission as consultants; Li Song, the director of the Folk Literature and Art Development Center of the Ministry of Culture as the chief editor; and 16 famous scholars as the members to organize, plan, select and determine the topics and determine the authors. After the establishment of the board, 50 famous experts and scholars in the field of festivals and the festival planners with extensive experiences have been invited to jointly edit the series.

The planning of the *Chinese Festival Culture Series* is to promote the traditional Chinese culture, explore the local and unique cultures, showcase the charms of the festivals of the Chinese Nation,

国务院新闻办公室的大力支持下，决定联合出版大型系列丛书——《中国节庆文化》丛书。为此，民族节庆专委会专门成立了《中国节庆文化》丛书编纂委员会，邀请了国际节庆协会（IFEA）主席兼首席执行官史蒂文·施迈德先生、中国文联执行副主席冯骥才先生、中国人类学民族学研究会常务副会长周明甫先生、国家民委政研室副主任兼中国人类学民族学研究会秘书长黄忠彩先生、国家民委文宣司司长武翠英女士等担任顾问，由文化部民族民间文艺发展中心主任李松担任主编，十六位知名学者组成编委会，负责丛书的组织策划、选题确定、体例拟定和作者的甄选。随后，组委会在全国范围内，遴选了五十位节庆领域知名专家学者以及有着丰富实操经验的节庆策划师共同编著。

策划《中国节庆文化》丛书，旨在弘扬中国传统文化，挖掘本土文化和独特文化，展示中华民族的节庆魅力，展现绚丽多姿的民俗风情，打造节庆城市形象。本丛书以对中国节庆文化感兴趣的中外读者为对象，以节庆活动为载体，向世界推广中国的传统文化和现代文化，让中国走向世界，让世界更了解中国。编委会要求每位参与编写者，力争做到理论性与实践性兼备，集专业性与通俗性于一体。

目前推出的是第一辑《春之节》，其编纂工作自2012年4月启动，2013年6月完成。期间编委会先后六次召开了专题会议，就丛书编纂体例、书目大纲、初稿、译稿与作者及译者进行研讨，共同修改完善书稿和译稿；就丛书的装帧设计、编辑风格、出版发行计划与出版社进行协商，集思广益，提高丛书的文化品位。

《春之节》共十册，分别介绍了中华大地上农历一月至三月有代表性的十个民族节庆，包括春节、元宵节、二月二、三月三、清明节、牡丹节、藏历年、壮族蚂蚜节、苗

express the gorgeous and colorful folk customs and create a festival image for cities. The target consumers of the series are the readers both at home and abroad who are interested in the festivals of China, and the purpose of the series is to promote the traditional culture and modern culture of China to the world and make the world know China in a better way by using the festivals as medium. The editorial board requests the editors shall integrate the theories into practice and balance the expertise and the popularity.

At present, the first part of the series will be published, namely the *Festivals in Spring*, and the editorial work of this part has been started in April, 2012 and completed in June, 2013. During this period of time, the editorial board has held six meetings to discuss with the authors and translators in terms of the compiling styles, outlines, first draft and translation to improve the draft and translation; and to consult with the publishing house in terms of the graphic design, editorial style and publishing schedule to improve the cultural quality of the series.

The first part *Festivals in Spring* is composed of 10 volumes to introduce 10 folk festivals of China from the first month to the third month of the Chinese Calendar, including the Spring Festival, the Lantern Festival, the Festival of February of the Second, the Festival of March the Third, the Tomb-Sweeping Day, the Peony Festival, the

Tibetan Calendar New Year, the Maguai Festival of the Zhuang People, the Sister Rice Festival, and the Saizhuang Festival of the Yi Ethnic Group. Each festival is introduced in detail to analyse its origin, development, distribution, customs, overseas dissemination and major activities, showing the readers a colorful picture about the Chinese festivals.

This series are the product of the cooperation between the Folk Festival Commission and the Anhui People's Publishing House. Anhui People's Publishing House is the first publishing house of its kind in Anhui Province, which has a history of more than 60 years, and has been in the leading position in terms of foreign publication. The Folk Festival Commission is the only organization at the national level in the field of the research of the Chinese festivals, which has rich expert resources and local festival resources. The series have integrated the advantageous resources of both parties. We will be delighted and gratified to see that the series could promote the foreign dissemination of the Chinese culture, promote the inheritance and preservation of the traditional and folk cultures, express the cultural charms of China and build the festival brand and image of China.

In deep meditation, the *Chinese Festival Culture Series* bears the wisdoms and knowledge of all of its authors and the great effort of the editors, and

族姊妹节、彝族赛装节等，对每个节日的起源与发展、空间流布、节日习俗、海外传播、现代主要活动形式等分别进行了详细的介绍和深度的挖掘，呈现给读者的将是一幅绚丽多彩的中华节庆文化画卷。

这套丛书的出版，是民族节庆专业委员会和安徽人民出版社合作的结晶。安徽人民出版社是安徽省最早的出版社，有六十余年的建社历史，在对外传播方面走在全国出版社的前列；民族节庆专业委员会是我国节庆研究领域唯一的国家级社团，拥有丰富的专家资源和地方节庆资源。这套丛书的出版，实现了双方优势资源的整合。丛书的面世，若能对推动中国文化的对外传播，促进传统民族文化的传承与保护，展示中华民族的文化魅力，塑造节庆的品牌与形象有所裨益，我们将甚感欣慰。

掩卷沉思，《中国节庆文化》丛书凝聚着诸位作者的智慧和学养，倾注着编纂者的心血和付出，也诠释着中华民族文化的灿烂与辉煌。在此，真诚感谢各位编委会成员、丛书作者、译者、出版社工作人员付出的辛勤劳动，以及各界朋友对丛书编纂工作的鼎力支持！希望各位读者对丛书多提宝贵意见，以便我们进一步完善后续作品，将更加璀璨的节庆文化呈现在世界面前。

《中国节庆文化》
丛书编委会
2013年12月

explains the splendid cultures of the Chinese Nation. We hereby sincerely express our gratitude to the members of the board, the authors, the translators, and the personnel in the publishing house for their great effort and to all friends from all walks of the society for their support. We hope you can provide your invaluable opinions for us to further promote the following work so as to show the world our excellent festival culture.

Editorial Board of
Chinese Festival Culture Series
December, 2013